MW00366585

Catch The
Christmas Spirit

And Keep It All Year Long

Also by Dorothy Wilhelm

No Assembly Required

The Pocket Book of Answers To Questions
You Never Got Around To Asking.

Catch The Christmas Spirit

And Keep It All Year Long

A collection of surprises, discoveries,
tips, and ideas

By Dorothy Wilhelm

NTL Editions

Never Too Late For Joyful Living Series

Copyright © 2014 by Dorothy Wilhelm

All rights reserved except for brief passages quoted in newspapers, magazine, radio or television reviews. No part of this book may be reproduced in any part or by any means electronic or mechanical, photocopying or recording, or by information storage and retrieval except by written permission from NTL Editions.

Published in the United States of America by NTL Editions
Printed in the United States
Never Too Late
PO Box 881
DuPont, WA 98327

ISBN paperback: 978-0-692-32974-0

Cover Design – Sue Balcer
Cover Photograph – Canstock photo
Text Design – Just Your Type.biz

First edition

Catch the Christmas Spirit 1. Christmas –reflection, tips, ideas, 2. Holiday ideas 3. Joyful living after 50.

Dedication

To my six children and their tribes
> Because you've been endlessly supportive
> And provided me with most of my material,
> Even if you won't let me use your names
> anymore
> Or Facebook entries. It's safe to say I wouldn't
> be a writer without all of you.

To Rebecca Morgan
> Without you, this book would have come out in
> July Of the year Never.

To Val
> For experienced advice and a kick when needed.

To everyone who ever said, "I read what you wrote.
> It Made me laugh."

Special Thanks to The News Tribune of Tacoma, WA where most of these columns first appeared.

Thank you for being my "flagship" newspaper home for two decades.

CONTENTS

You Were Expecting
Maybe Santa Claus?

Dear (Please fill in your name, which you know better than I do, but make it something affectionate because I'm pretty sure that if I met you we'd like each other.)

Anyway, I'm writing this because I love Christmas, and I'm betting you do too. But look, let's level here. Christmas has changed. All of the holidays have. For most of us it can't be the same old day. No use trying to sit on Santa's lap. He can be quite unpleasant about it.

So it's up to us, who have passed our fifties, or our sixties, or – well never mind – it's up to us to look for the light at the end of the tunnel, and hope it's not a train. Clerks often tell me, as I leave their store, "You have a wonderful evening now." Usually I inform them that the last wonderful evening I had was in Nashville in 1998. That isn't strictly true. I'm having a pretty good time right now.

We can have wonderful holidays. We can have a wonderful life. If you are having a wonderful life, then we should share our secrets. So here are my ideas, and I'd love to hear yours. To paraphrase Humphrey Bogart in Casablanca, "This could be the beginning of a beautiful friendship."

Contact me at www.itsnevertoolate.com, or Dorothy@itsnevertoolate.com or PO Box 881, DuPont, WA 98327.

Santa Doesn't Call Here Any More

Santa doesn't call at our house anymore. I know. I have Caller ID. If the Jolly Old Elf called here, it would squeal on him even if he didn't leave a message. Nope. Santa hasn't been around, and frankly I can already tell I'll have just a little trouble getting the Christmas spirit this year. I'm the one who is out of step, I think. I had a friend once who left a party early. "I had to leave," she recalled. "I was boring." "You mean the party was boring?" She reflected a minute and shook her head. "No. No, it was me, definitely. I was boring." Well, it's that way for me. I may have to skip Christmas this year. I'm boring.

In our neighborhood, the joyous season officially starts with the arrival of Charlie the Wonder Salesman, bringing the rolls of Christmas wrap he sold us way back in September. He also delivers our attractive selections of Yucky Yule Candy, stuck together in their four-color lithographed tins, and little boxes of Pretty Awful Tasting Christmas Nuts. Every nine days he arrives with the latest shipment of whatever he's selling to raise funds for school or church. Charlie is a heck of a salesman. He is 11. There used to be a Charlie in my house. She's a nurse and lives in Maryland now.

Christmases change. That's my recurrent theme, I guess. Over the years our family built a holiday tradition that felt right. We made cookies and burned them, frosted them anyway, got frosting on noses, fingers and earlobes. We did crafts, read stories, lit candles, sang songs. I can personally show you 93 things to do with an empty roll of toilet paper and a full roll of scotch tape. Martha Stewart, eat your heart out.

We believed in Christmas miracles. The year the *Star Wars* movie came out, there were no *Star Wars* toys available at Christmas. The manufacturers announced kids would find gift certificates under the tree. Our family and friends sat up nights recreating the complete movie cast from odd bits of action figures, papier-mâché and cloth. This required great ingenuity. Obi-Wan Kenobi was pieced together in a dorm room at the

University of Washington. An x-wing fighter, magnificent with slightly droopy wings, took shape in our basement. On Christmas morning eight year old Patrick was the only child in America, as far as we knew, to wake up to a complete set of Star Wars figures, and we all felt our spirits soar, along with the X-Wing.

The holidays are definitely more challenging each year. You're urged to choose your Grandchild's gift from an electronic toy registry. Barbie's getting a body transformation, and the newest revision of *The New Joy of Cooking* is almost too heavy to lift. I may have to rent a three-year-old just so I can feel what Christmas is really like again.

When you're past fifty you may have to start all over again to create a holiday that fits. Easier said than done. I found advice that made sense to me in Janet Luher's book, *The Guide to Simple Living*. Her suggestion: "Make a plan with the people with whom you will celebrate Christmas. Remove what no longer works; but for everything you remove you must put something back that does fit."

Begin by taking out the things that no longer work. That would be the too big tree, the parties that no longer matter. "Add new things that fit." I'm auditioning a whole list of possible new traditions. I tried Contra dancing. Fast, fun, it has nothing to do with South America. Something apparently that was danced in the colonies. On the turns, partners are supposed to look into each other's eyes. My batteries have been charging ever since the dance Saturday night. I'm singing in a Latin Chant Choir. It's quite satisfying. Somehow in Latin, it's harder to tell that a person can't sing. I have a friend who treated herself to a facelift. It cost $6,500. I'm not quite that depressed. I did color my hair a nice Christmas red. It's a wonderful shade which never occurred spontaneously anywhere in nature. I don't even have to wonder if people believe it's my real color. By the way, redheads do have more fun.

Last year at the radio station where I broadcast, the engineer, age 24, played what he called Christmas classics to introduce the segments of my show. "You'll love these," he enthused. "These are real classics from the old days." His old days turned out to go back no further than "Rocking Around the Christmas Tree."

This year I'm taking no chances. I'm bringing my own music. Maybe that's the blueprint for a successful holiday season, past fifty. Take no chances, and carry your own music with you. When you hear Bing Crosby, and Perry Como, No Place like Home for The Holidays and White Christmas, I'll smile at you and you smile back. I've got the music and they're playing our songs.

Christmas - 1998

Codfish Soup

My mother made Codfish Soup on Christmas Eve. Every Christmas Eve. It featured chunks of dried cod and an occasional bay leaf swimming through a gelatinous tomato broth of uncertain origin. This unique dish was made from a secret family recipe developed by my Great Grandmother in Italy. I can't imagine why. It was terrible luck not to eat this soup on Christmas Eve, my mother insisted. It wasn't such good luck to eat it either, let me tell you. This stuff was really, really awful, I thought. I used to dread Christmas Eve because of it. I miss that soup. Christmas isn't the same without it. It's extraordinary how many Christmas traditions are like that. You don't miss them till they're gone.

Remember the year Rudolph the Red Nosed Reindeer was born? I suppose not, but I do. Montgomery Ward gave a booklet with that story to every child who visited Santa. I had no idea that I was present at the birth of a legend but it I knew it was a great story and we all wanted it. Sort of like

Pokémon with antlers. That was the year Mother visited Santa, too. A visit to Santa was very traumatic for me, but I had to go to get the book. Then I stared horrified as my mother perched on Santa's furry lap. "A pair of nylons, please," Mother whispered. In the forties, ladies did without nylons, of course, proudly painting their legs and adding an eyebrow pencil seam down the back, but the real thing would be heaven and it would take a miracle to get them. "Oh, my dear" Santa laughed. "Mrs. Claus told me not to come back to the North Pole if I didn't bring her a pair, and I can't find them anywhere."

This was bad news. I was no dummy. I was pretty sure he wasn't the real Santa and probably this was another of those grown-up jokes. But still. If Santa couldn't even get Mrs. Santa what she wanted, that meant I was pretty much on my own.

I have come to another year like that, I think, where I have to reframe my attitude toward my celebration and traditions. This seems to happen uncomfortably often. For instance, I've always insisted on a Christmas tree that pushed against the ceiling and filled the whole room with fragrance. That takes the efforts of at least two people and a lot of engineering. Last year I had to call Rent A Son to help me get the tree down. This season I have to do something different.

There are many possibilities, of course. My friend Patsy is thinking about spending the holiday in a hotel. "None of my children are speaking to each other," she explains. Cruises are fashionable for Christmas but another friend recalled, "Last Christmas, I went on the cruise from hell. No hot water, and they couldn't get the air conditioning off." Attractive as that sounds, I think I'll skip it.

Perhaps I need to meet new people. In desperation, I tried the singles line on the Internet again. When I answered an ad from a man who said he was a writer, he sent me a story about The Stork That Brought The Baby Jesus. I'm sorry. I've got six kids. I'm not buying that.

Now I know someone is going to scold me for not planning volunteer activities or serving Christmas dinner at a shelter. Those are great ideas, and well worth a mention, but sometimes you have to try something just a little outrageous.

If all else fails, give yourself a new slant on life. My mother had the answer to that, too. She rejuvenated herself and her outlook by lying on a slant board with cucumber slices over her eyes for ten minutes. You don't own a slant board? The ironing board, leaning against the bed will do. Mother still used this trick until she was nearly 80, but I freely admit that it's become just a little risky for me to be clambering onto the ironing board. Besides, I haven't seen my ironing board in at least three years. It's around here somewhere.

Let me see. What can I do that I've never done before? Dancing lessons? Maybe a trip to Vienna? Why not? At least I'll pick up a few travel brochures. It's amazing what comes to mind when your eyes are covered with cucumber slices. Maybe I will just make some Codfish Soup. Probably not, though.

Note: I did make Codfish Soup for a Christmas party given by friends who begged me to do so. I had to search quite a bit to find dried cod, and the soup was every bit as awful as I remembered. I didn't see how I could possibly take it to the party. So I put a little wine in and cooked it awhile. That was better. So I added a little more wine and it was pretty good. By the time I took it to the party, there were about two bottles of wine in the soup and it was delicious. I had to stand in front of the soup to keep the kids from tasting it. I was awarded a set of gourmet kitchen tools for my effort. I never made Codfish Soup again.

Christmas - 1999

Cardboard Stars

My mother never let me cut out the cardboard stars for our Christmas tree, not even one. With my fat five-year-old hands, I couldn't cut straight edges and these stars covered with tin foil had to be perfect. Each year my Dad searched for the biggest tree he could find to cut and it was always so huge it seemed to burst out of the tiny main room of our little shack near the banks of Montana's cold Kootenai River. On this night, Dad had cut the tree for us before he went out to his shift on the railroad section gang. Our walls, covered with old newspapers for decoration and warmth, did very little to keep out the cold. So a sweater, a coat, and a constant runny nose were my winter weather accessories. Snow pushed half way up the windows and without electricity or running water, we had a long dark winter ahead of us. I didn't care! It never occurred to me that anyone else lived differently.

"Let me hang a star on the tree," I begged.

The huge tree sparkling with stars and tin foil icicles filled the cold house with scent and beauty was the most gorgeous thing I'd ever seen. I thought this every year. I still do. I would always have a Christmas tree exactly like this one, I told myself!

Five years later, just at the beginning of World War II, practically the whole town of Warland moved to Spokane, Washington. We went with them, and traditions changed. Our tree in the tiny upstairs railroad apartment was much smaller, but it still had the cardboard stars and tin foil icicles. We had electricity in the house, and while many trees in the neighborhood had lights on their trees, that was not for the likes of us. Mrs. Nichols, the landlady, was given to sweeping upstairs at any hour of the day or night, and turning off all the lights. It was very disquieting.

Two years later, in a cracker box of a house, shared with an incredibly large colony of mice, there were electric lights on the tree for the first time. Electricity came into our house efficiently through the black thick cord that hung down from each ceiling light fixture--it wasn't so much a fixture as a naked bulb, but I found the light fascinating. It was very educational. I learned that if you stuck a hairpin in the end of the switch, it made all the lights go out and your arm felt like it was going to sleep and then it really hurt. The tree was not as big as the Montana tree, but the lights looked like little glass candles and as they warmed up, they began to bubble magically in red and orange and green. I will always have lights just like this on my Christmas tree, I promised myself.

In my own home, for nearly thirty years it was my turn to preside over one perfect Christmas after another, and I was the one who got to say what was perfect! Anyone and anything that couldn't move, or couldn't move fast enough, was cleaned, moved, sprayed or decorated. We didn't have celebrations so much as theatrical productions. "Don't stage manage, Mom" the boys cautioned--but I never listened. I was the Queen of Christmas, wearing red and green earrings made from glass Christmas balls so big that if they had broken they would have slashed my jugular vein. This was my time of year, and I loved it. The tree had to be big enough to scrape paint off the living room ceiling when we put it in place. One year, in fact, we put a piece of black jagged poster board in the living room over the tree, with a smaller tree just above it on the roof, so it looked as if the tree were bursting through. I thought that was just about right.

One year in an excess of Yuletide spirit, I actually spray painted everything in my path gold. This included a dozen artichokes (for a centerpiece), the kids' Legos, (Christmas castle) and the dog. I don't recommend that, though. It turned out the dog really didn't appreciate it. It all culminated in a grand Christmas Eve procession with everyone taking part. Sir played Christmas hymns on the small Hammond organ with all of us singing and carrying figures from the nativity scene to their place in the Christmas story. Then Sir died, and everything had to change. Those changes didn't come easily. It seemed important to us to do things we'd never done before, which is why one year we ordered pepperoni pizza and watched Harrison Ford in "Raiders of the Lost Ark." That did not work out as well as you might think.

Now it's time to make new traditions again, and as always, it's not easy. The children are grown and don't get home often at Christmas. I hardly recognize the young man in Navy uniform as the little boy who once waited breathlessly for Santa to leave him a jet airplane. He now has a rime of frost on his dark hair and is close to retirement from a career of flying real planes.

The trick is not to look back longingly to that magical cold Montana Christmas, but instead to create small new traditions that bring the same delight as those long ago trees and bubbling lights.

I am experimenting with cutting back. I haven't decided whether to have a tree this year, because if you put up a tree, you have to take it down again right away, at least by February. I have found, though, that if you leave it up until Valentine's Day, it turns a nice, satisfactory red that fits in with the season.

My outdoor decorations are certainly less elaborate this year. I have three strings of lights and a tulip tree in the front yard. When the lights are on the tree--which is, say, from December 19 to, oh, May 23--we are decorated for Christmas.

When the lights are not on the tree, we aren't.

So far, my best new tradition is to warm two bathrobes in the dryer, put them on, one over the other, and curl up with a mug of hot chocolate with--and this is important--two marshmallows. I have a two foot tall figure of the Grinch which dances on his hands and sings. It's in the poorest possible taste, but it makes me giggle. So that's a new tradition--at least until the batteries die.

Friends and family have become most important--the ones who are here, and the ones who can never be again. A reader wrote that her new tradition is to decorate her small tree just with family pictures, instead of Christmas balls. Giving unexpected gifts is a good new tradition. The World Vision Catalog (www.worldvisiongifts.org) says that for only $15.00 I could give two rabbits to an impoverished family, and in a year they'd have 50 rabbits. Imagine. You can give a whole sheep for $126.00. I like that kind of optimism.

Some traditions never change. I still can't cut straight edges for cardboard stars. Sometimes we just have to let go of the old memories and start a new journey. Are we there yet?

Note #1: Bubble lights for Christmas trees were born in 1935, invented by Carl Otis. They couldn't be manufactured during WWII, so they became really popular in 1945, which was the year we had them on our tree.

Note #2: Sir was my semi-playful name for my husband. He was a regular Army career officer, and the joke was "He allowed me to call him by his first name, but he certainly didn't encourage it. He preferred 'Sir' in moments of passion."

Christmas – 2003

Tradition!

I hated to visit my grandmother's house, Christmas or not. Even if you made it over the river and through the woods, you still had a three-mile trek straight uphill to Grandma's rugged ranch house in rural Oregon. There was no electricity or plumbing, but there seemed to be an impressive catalog of living and none too friendly critters like spiders and bats in the corners of the attic where I slept.

Grandma, being incredibly old (about the age I am now), had a very large china "chamber pot" under her bed, so that she didn't have to attempt the half block walk to the outhouse in the middle of the night. Her wall was plastered with pictures of the saints cut out of Catholic calendars for about fifty years. Apparently they were subjects of contemplation while she was thus occupied. I could never see how you could sit on the teeny tiny rim, anyway. It turned out that Grandma preferred to carry the vessel out into the living room for extended use, since she was embarrassed to have the saints observe her in such an improper activity.

Before we get too sentimental about changing times, I've got to admit there are plenty of Christmas traditions like those visits I just don't miss.

I don't miss Codfish Soup on Christmas Eve, and I don't miss the unending line of visitors--aunts, uncles and cousins who all seemed, unaccountably, to need to be kissed. "Give Aunt Manny and Aunt Vi a kiss now," my mother would prompt, indicating people I didn't even recognize. Aunt Vi was ok. She was young and cute and fun. Aunt Manny wasn't and she had a bristly mustache. The newly arrived company quickly grabbed the preferred sleeping places. And if a bed already had three or four aunts sleeping in it, we smaller children had to sleep across the foot of the bed, dodging hard feet all through the night... And to tell the truth, I was none too crazy about my grandmother, either. I thought she smelled funny, and I couldn't understand her heavily accented English. She was given to singing loudly while hitting a tambourine with hip and elbow. Altogether, I thought she was the most embarrassing woman God ever put on this earth. I really couldn't see why I couldn't have Christmas with just my Mom and Dad, especially since Santa Claus seemed to have a lot of trouble finding us even when we were home. But my mother always insisted that family is most important, especially at Christmas time. And by family, she apparently met the whole range of scratchy and embarrassing uncles and aunts.

I'd like to say that as years went on, I developed an admiration for this remarkable woman, as I learned how she had come from Italy to the tenements of Chicago bearing twelve children and burying three along the way. But that didn't happen. When my Uncle Lou came home from the Navy, he brought Grandma a monkey which she carried about on her back. She seemed a little more interesting after that, but I was excessively young and dumb and not given to looking beneath the surface. It's not always possible to like the people we're supposed to love.

There are things I miss. I miss thick Christmas catalogs, and animated downtown window displays.

I miss old fashioned Christmas stockings. You hung up any fairly clean sock which some time during the night would magically be filled with an orange at the toe, apple at the heel, a few nuts and hard candy, and maybe a candy cane or two. You had to be cautious putting your hand into the stocking, though. There was always the danger that some sibling or cousin, infused with Yuletide wit, would stuff the stocking with rabbit droppings in the hope they'd be mistaken for jelly beans. Sometimes it worked.

I miss the wonderful gifts from department store Santas. In those days, Santa gave wonderful gifts, not one of those pathetic two-inch candy canes they give kids today. I stood in line two years in a row for one of the coveted first editions of Robert May's poem, *Rudolph the Red Nosed Reindeer*. Montgomery Ward made them available, and we never guessed that Rudolph would be with us our whole lives. I wish I'd kept the books.

When I left my little Grandson after a visit last fall, I said, "I'll try to come back for Christmas." He threw his arm across his eyes in a world-weary gesture. "Oh, I hope not. Too many people,"

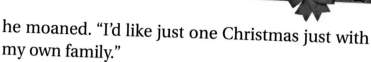

he moaned. "I'd like just one Christmas just with my own family."

Ah. Surprised at first, and maybe a little hurt, I remembered the unending line of aunts and cousins. Tradition is what you make it after all. "I'll come in the spring instead," I said--"and maybe I'll bring a monkey."

Christmas – 2011

They're Buying Back Their Toys

It's Christmas again. There's a cold tang in the air, carols on the radio and our adult children are sitting in front of their computer screens trying to buy back their toys. I'm talking about the ones that we made them give away 20 years ago: G.I. Joe and Barbie, Liddle Kiddles and Major Matt Mason.

See for yourself. Log on the Internet at ebay. com and choose from 800,000 of those nearly forgotten toys in 1,000 categories. Each is looking for a new home with the highest bidder. There are 100 listings for G.I. Joe alone. Barbies are the pricey items, though. The Harley Barbie goes for about $100, and an original Barbie brought $4,200.

My son just paid $14 for a Major Matt Mason figure. It is quite nice. It is missing one hand, but if it'd had both hands it would have cost at least $52. Major Matt had a tendency to lose hands anyway. The kids went around impaling each other on the wire stumps. Sentimental experiences like that can't be taken lightly.

I know how this got started, and it's partly my fault. I want to acknowledge that right now. It's probably your fault, too. We're the ones who made those impressionable youngsters give their toys away and thus scarred their little lives.

For me, it all goes back to that long ago Christmas when I gathered my six kids around me and talked about the less fortunate children in our community. I implored each of my brood to pick a favorite toy to share, since they were sure to get more. Lots more.

With six kids, the brightly wrapped piles of toys towered sky high. The older kids, wise in the ways of the world, and their mother, had prepared for this predictable moment by gathering belongings that, to put it kindly, had passed their prime. One daughter, who chooses to remain anonymous, got extra points for giving away a perfect baby doll in absolutely pristine condition with all of its little wardrobe complete. It even had both hands. I didn't find out until much later that this foresighted young person didn't like babies, even doll babies, and was delighted at the opportunity to send this plastic bundle of joy on its way.

Somehow, the G.I. Joes and Major Matt Masons disappeared or were given away--or maybe they disintegrated. But they were missed. Our younger daughter, who is involved with the real business of survival in her own apartment this year, observes with some asperity, "Judging from the missing fingers and limbs, all of our G.I. Joes were either involved in some nasty hazings or had a mass run-in with the mob. Maybe they were all taken for a ride."

Christmas has changed a lot at my house. I am not even sure I'll have a tree this year. Last year's tree was too big. The trunk cracked the tree stand. Water pooled in hitherto undiscovered crevices all over the hardwood floor. I had to call Rent-A-Son to clean up the mess.

Most of my friends are looking for new ways to celebrate the season. Time to try something different. Maybe a cruise or a trip to Taos. "It's getting harder and harder for the children to come home, and I just don't want them worrying about me," said one friend.

I don't want to go anywhere. I want something wonderful to happen right here.

I have lots of dreams I haven't used yet. This is a great time to do something we just never had the time or the courage to try before. So the last few weeks I've been dusting off a favorite dream. If the kids can get back their toys, why can't I?

It seems to me that I used to love to dress up, to put on beautiful clothes, Lace, satin. Feathers. Jewels. Real diamonds, and become a character from another world.

So you won't find me sitting home feeling lonely this Christmas. You see, I've become a showgirl. No, don't laugh. I'll be out at the Puyallup Fairgrounds in a new production called "The Stardust Follies." I'll be dancing, and, heaven help us, singing. I am empowered to sing any songs with a vocal range of three notes or less. So let the kids sit in front of the computer screen this Christmas. If they can take back a little of their own, I'll cheer them on. And I hope--no, I know--they'll be there cheering for me when I make my debut.

Christmas is still a magic time, if only we choose to make our own magic.

Note #1 – In 2014 the Harley Barbie with Ken was listed on eBay for $380. But then the Barbie Harley motor-cycle is $372. These are remote control toys. I do not know what they remotely control.
Major Matt Mason with both hands is $99.

Note#2 – I'm sorry to say that my debut in "Stardust Follies" was not what you'd call a success. But I did have some great pictures made with a collection of five men. That's not likely to happen again.

Christmas – 1998

The Perfect Gift

My battered purse hangs from my shoulder by one shredded strap, held in two places by pins. Last week a lady stopped me to ask if I'd been attacked by a pack of wild dogs or simply been the victim of a mugging. "Neither," I replied with dignity. "This is a designer bag. It's meant to look like this!" That isn't exactly true. But it was a gift and I just can't bring myself to throw my gifts away. Let's face it, I can't throw anything away, but if someone goes to the trouble of choosing a gift for me, wrapping it, and presenting it, that item is guaranteed a place in my heart and home forever.

Now that downsizing has struck, the carol heard most often this year begins "For heavens' sake Mother, aren't you ever going to throw anything away?" No. No, I'm not. But thanks for asking.

Only this evening, one of the children who shall be nameless to protect me, told me with some asperity that it's time I think in terms of disposable gifts. I should expect things I can eat or use up, like fruitcake or personalized toilet paper, I suppose. Or maybe have a goat given in my name to a starving village. And I could do that. But I'd still want to keep the gifts I already have.

I blame it on growing up in Montana. I know a couple of folks who grew up in Montana and are pretty normal but unfortunately none of them are me. Our small town was without electricity, water, or shopping. So we made each other meaning-ful gifts. Like Aprons or ashtrays. The guys looked funny in the aprons and hardly anybody smoked but it was the thought that counted. The trick was to avoid Mrs. Evans' special gift of her own home-made dill pickles that seemed to have been aged in kerosene. We couldn't eat the pickles but the kerosene was very good for killing potato bugs. We learned to nicely thank the donor and cher-ish the gift, sort of a like a portable hug. When my own family came along, we encouraged the chil-dren to give last year's toys away to make room for the gifts that would surely be coming. That worked until the year my daughter flatly refused to give away her baby doll after another new real

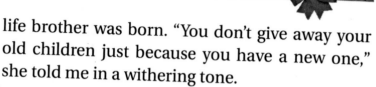

life brother was born. "You don't give away your old children just because you have a new one," she told me in a withering tone.

I know of one father who is considering asking grandparents to contribute to the children's college fund instead of choosing a conventional gift. I sure hope they won't do that. Gift giving is so much fun for grandparents. You just can't get down and roll around on the floor with a bank deposit book. We found one workable solution. On Christmas day only a few gifts were opened and the rest were kept to be opened and enjoyed one or two a day, throughout the twelve days of Christmas. One day might be for board games; another for books; one day might be for a trip to the children's museum with Grandma. There was always a "welcome home from the first day back to school" gift that might be as small as a personalized pencil. On Twelfth Night, we turned on all the lights for the last time, and our rich Christmas season was officially over.

I hope I never downsize so much that I can't keep the most important memories with me. I like the idea of spending each of the days of this holiday sharing something special with the people I care about and perhaps passing some memories on.

Some gifts match the wonder of the season. No gift can outshine the new baby grandson in our family. And for the gifts that were lost or taken away, our hearts are heavy but we have to believe there's always got to be a star out there somewhere, just for them.

Christmas - 2001

Angel Unaware

On the night before Christmas, I awoke to hear something hitting the roof. Hard. It was definitely not Santa and his reindeer. Instead of the prancing and pawing of each little hoof, there was just one big loud repeated thump, alternated with an even louder Ker-Thunk. I shook my husband awake. "It's just the angel," he said, struggling to turn over and go back to sleep. He was talking about the life size angel I had painstakingly constructed and hung for display as the high light of our holiday celebration. This was very bad news for me.

In retrospect, I must ask, who knows what's life size for an angel? This angel was a little over five feet tall, with a six foot wing span. She was built for flying, not walking. She was blowing triumphantly on a golden trumpet and she was made of papier-mâché. The angel hung between the faux pillars of our faux colonial home in Dayton, Ohio that Christmas and at that moment, she was out there engaged in beating her faux brains out.

I have to admit that I am addicted to papier-mâché construction. I have been, ever since the Christmas I was given a volume called *The Big Blue Book for Girls* when I was twelve. It purported to contain everything a girl should know. Surprisingly, one of those things was papier-mâché construction, a popular Depression era craft.

You can make anything out of papier-mâché, I learned. You can make jewelry. Jewelry boxes. Hors d'oeuvre trays. Fake food to fill the trays. You can even make furniture. But most of all, you can create art. I was hooked for life by all that can be built from a pile of newspaper strips with flour and water that will never see the inside of the gravy boat. When my Number Three Son was five and fell in love with Oscar the Grouch, I made him his very own set of custom designed garbage cans from paper mash. They were painted silver and he loved them. When Number Four Son wanted a Noah's ark, his Dad built the ark in his wood shop while I papier-mâché'd the whole Noah's family, complete with Mr. and Mrs. Noah, sons, wives and babies. It all comes around, though. This year, my Grandson wants a Noah's Ark Playmobile. $100.

I'm not sure this is progress.

Admit it now, aren't the unexpected things the best part of every holiday? When the kids were little, the great holiday treat was waiting for the Christmas catalogs to arrive. Of course, in those days they didn't come in handcarts as they do now. So many catalogs have arrived this year that if they ever do abandon the space program, we can make a good start getting to the moon, just stacking up those catalogs and climbing on them. But in the days when only two catalogs came (Wards and Sears) each child was given a different color crayon (this was before marking pens) and allowed to circle absolutely every toy that appealed to them in any way. The pages came out looking like rainbows, but it kept them busy long enough for us to have a meal or two in peace. Now I know you're going to want to lecture me about the real spirit of Christmas being giving. We'll get to that. But if it makes a person feel rich to imagine owning absolutely everything in a catalog, why not? They knew, the strict rule was that in the end, they must pick just one thing to ask for their real present.

And then, that long ago Christmas, I had my great inspiration. I'd been stuck indoors with the four kids all winter, as usual. I was pregnant, as usual, when I saw the picture of a renaissance angel and visualized a spectacular Christmas display, built by my own hands that would have the whole neighborhood talking. It certainly did.

From September until December, most of the dining room was covered with a plastic tarp. The floor had newspaper inadvertently but permanently glued to it. The children hung over the baby gate I'd put at the door, surviving on peanut butter sandwiches and begging me to come out. The angel was finished in time for Christmas. She was splendid hanging from a brass ring in the middle of her back with her six foot wingspan and her jubilant trumpet. Until the wind started to blow. What I hadn't foreseen was that the space between the faux pillars made a perfect wind tunnel and my angel was truly airborne. She bounced up. She gyrated down. There was no stopping her. We all piled into our winter coats and trailed outside to watch her go. The children were ecstatic at this unexpected retribution for the months of neglect and the neighbors were appreciative of the entertainment, although they weren't so crazy about waking in the middle of the night to see it. I was aghast. Each time the angel swung around, she whammed her triumphant trumpet into the roof. It hung at a dejected angle.

And the roof didn't look so good, either.

We've all had craft projects that didn't work out as expected. When my children were married, I tenderly sculpted each of them charming little papier-mâché portrait figures of themselves, which they all seem to have misplaced Still, I love the idea of making something from absolutely nothing--unless you count a floor refinishing and a touch of roof repair.

I've learned my lesson. Anything can be overdone. And yet, lately I've been thinking that maybe a papier-mâché angel--a small one-- would look great hanging between the pillars on my front porch. I wonder what my Resident Home Owners Association rules say about that.

Note #1 – They said no.

Christmas - 2010

Off With Their Heads!

My son and his wife shoveled snow for six hours on Christmas day, during what was called Minnesota's worst winter storm in thirty years. You know it's a bad storm when Minnesota churches cancel services and other events are called off because of snow. Generally, in Minnesota, they just tighten up the scarf, put on the mittens and keep shoveling. I helped out by documenting the event with my new digital camera. I am still at the "off with their heads" stage, and I couldn't focus in the snow, but there's a nice picture of the shovel handle and hands. Being certifiably wimpy, and from the Northwest, where "you don't have to shovel rain" I was allowed to stay in the house with my two little grandsons. We demonstrated solidarity by watching "Ice Age 3."

A snow blower is high on the family wish list. With their current household budget it will take about five years to save up for a good heavy duty one. That means that when the next decade arrives, they'll be able to reminisce and say, "Remember back in 2009 when we had to dig out of that big winter storm by hand?"

I am sure they will do this, because it is the custom as the decade changes to look back over the past ten years and try to make some sense of it all. Newspapers do it. Dave Barry does it. My turn now.

Ten years ago, I confessed that I was not computer literate, not yet on the Internet Highway. In fact, I was not even at the first bus stop. I had plenty of company. Today, the biggest use of the Internet is driven by those of us over 55, and I spend a couple of hours a day in front of my 22" monitor, just keeping up.

In July of 2000 I wrote about a brand new assisted living facility which opened in downtown Tacoma, WA. It made headlines and a big hit with the adult children of prospective residents by offering only "heart healthy foods." A special chef was imported who would cook and serve only what was good for the new residents. This paradise of perfect nutrition lasted exactly 10 days. Then there was a near riot. Residents were not satisfied with perfect food. They wanted pizza. They wanted tacos, and they wanted junk food. And they got it.

Over the past ten years, most mail has come in response to columns about health issues--and the frog, of course. In January of 2000 I wrote about my TIA (transient ischemic attack some-times called a "mini stroke") and urged everyone to create and carry a list of all of the medications they take and what they're taking it for--and see that family members have a copy. I also urged them to list contact people so hours won't be lost trying to find out who to call, as it was for me. "It may seem that we're now talking about carrying a document roughly the size of the first draft of *War and Peace*," I wrote, "But a report released by the National Center for Health Statistics showed that Washington has the seventh-highest stroke death rate in the country." (This state has now dropped to thirteenth).

A report released in 2000 said that the group of people 55 years of age and older owned 77% of all the financial assets in America. That's still about the same. Not me, of course. All of my assets are tied up in under eye concealer and sculpting mascara.

The years ahead look very uncertain, but yesterday I held my eight-day-old Great Grandson, while his big brother looked on proudly. I took out my new digital camera to capture the moment. Click. Missed his head. Click. Missed the brother. Click. Got part of the dog. Click. At last. Baby and brother! Now, take the camera and get a picture of me with the baby, please.

When 2020 comes and this little boy will be ten years old, Great Grandma Dorothy, if luck and health hold, will have these pictures and memories to share. "That's you, Darling, I'll say, "and that's Great Grandma holding you. I know you can't see my head, but it's not important. I wasn't using it anyway."

Christmas - 2009

Those Who Think Young

"You mustn't think of yourself as 80 years old," the very large lady insisted. "You're 80 years Young," She said it like "Younnnnng," as if she were bestowing a prize. I inspected the three inches of extra heavy support hose showing between my pants hem and orthopedic shoes. I politely stifled a burp of acid reflux. I haven't just been touched by time. I've been molested. "No," I replied thoughtfully, "I'm pretty sure that's 80 years *old*."

It's true. By the time we meet again, I will have passed that big 80th birthday complete with champagne toasts and a gathering of my whole clan. And you know something? I'm tickled pink. How lucky I am to be able to look back, and know that I've been part of some of the most turbulent years of history of our country. It isn't just something I read. I remember the kerfuffle (definitely not a word in 1941) when President Roosevelt moved Thanksgiving Day. I remember the jostling crowds on VJ day, when WWII was over. I'll never forget the bleak November morning when a phone call came from half a world away that our young president had been assassinated. I am touched, still, by the memory of lines of Taiwanese and Chinese people who came to comfort the American community at that time of our terrible loss and the Mass for President Kennedy offered in Mandarin at the mission church that night.

There's a popular belief that no matter how many decades have gone by, it's mandatory to concentrate on appearing and feeling young. But I don't think we should turn our backs on the gifts we've been given just because the wrapping on the package is now a bit wrinkled. Instead, we should try to add new experiences.

I never expected to be a teacher, but for the past three months I have been teaching public speaking at Clover Park Technical College, filling in while the regular instructor, Dr. Phil Venditti, is on sabbatical. I am just blown away by the caliber of the students and their determination to create a better life for themselves, their families and their communities. Many are military veterans and single parents. Most hold a job as well as going to school. This isn't a carefree campus experience for most of them. This is a hard fought battle, and they're determined to take that last hill with honors.

The classes started with an "Elevator Speech." That's where you find yourself in an elevator with someone who turns toward you and says, "What do you do?" Before the doors open on the third floor, you must answer so compellingly that this potential employer asks to hear more. Community business people have been invited to share this experience.

One speech was about significant people in the students' lives, and we cried together as they spoke of love remembered and love lost.

In one demonstration speech, a student reprised his military experience to show us how to conduct a search for a suspected terrorist. The student demonstrator honored my dinosaur sensibility by using his subject's armpit to simulate a "crotch search." "I certainly appreciated that," the "suspect" said. Me too.

We learned to make green smoothies. Kale is everywhere.

We learned to give CPR. "Are you all right, sir?" the student medic inquired of his patient/mannequin, and then played ventriloquist to turn his head and answer for the patient in a tiny, piping voice, "No. No, I'm not."

The old song says it best. "If you become a teacher, by your pupils you'll be taught." In these times when we're constantly connected by technology, I've been honored to be touched by these amazing people.

So Merry Christmas to the students of Public Speaking classes 0517 and 0518 at Clover Park Technical College. Thank you for the gifts of yourself, and--okay, I admit it--thanks for teaching me how to think young.

Bring on those birthdays! After all, an antique is something 100 or more years old, so I have lots of time. There it is in black and white. I'm not an antique. I'm a collectible.

Christmas/Birthday - 2013

First Christmas

This was the First Christmas in my new, smaller home. Under the high ceilings, there's plenty of room for a lovely, tall Christmas tree. Unfortunately in this mini space, there's only width for a branch spread of 6 inches. My children urged an artificial tree. They snap together in seconds and really you can't tell them from real ones. (The trees, not the children.) These trees have the lights already attached and pop open like pup tents. They pointed out that even Martha Stewart has given her name to a line of artificial trees. I was unmoved. There's something about the splendor of a real evergreen filling the room with the scent of pine. In our early years, Sir and I took all of the furniture out of our bedroom and put the tree in there and behind a secure baby gate at the door. We enjoyed the tree and our toddlers at the same time. There's still something about bringing a live tree into the house that transports me back to my growing up years in Montana.

In those holiday seasons, the radio brought

Christmas into the clear, cold days. From the time I was three years old, the days to Christmas were measured by the radio adventures of the Cinnamon Bear and his wimpy friends, Judy and Jimmy. Together, each day, they searched for the special Silver Star that traditionally topped their Christmas tree. If they couldn't find the star and the Crazy Quilt Dragon who stole it, well, it just wouldn't be Christmas.

I thought of the Cinnamon Bear often during this downsized holiday season because I couldn't find my Christmas ornaments. I can't find a lot of things now that you ask.

The sad fact is that Santa had to forget about cookies when he visited this year. I can't find my cookie sheets and I haven't even found my salt and pepper shakers yet. But the real truth is that I still can't bring myself to bake in my dazzling clean oven. To make matters worse, my neighbors' homes blossomed with twinkling lights as each one vied to be named the best-decorated house in the neighborhood. Naturally, I couldn't find my lights. There might as well have been an arrow to my darkened porch saying, "Ms. Scrooge lives here!"

I did cook a real meal for my son's birthday. I had postponed this as long as possible. I didn't want to get my new kitchen dirty but you can't live on cheese and crackers forever. It went surprisingly well, except that I could only find the beaters, but not my mixer and I had promised my son a cake. I discovered that if you hold a beater in each hand and make really fast arm circles in a big bowl, you can whip up a pretty decent chocolate cake. I wouldn't want to do it every day, but it is good aerobic exercise. The cake was sort of like a puffy pancake

When you downsize, you have to downsize your holiday celebration, too. It's a good time to try something really new. You can ask Ginger Passarelli for ideas about that. Ginger lives in the tiny mining town of Black Diamond, Washington, but spends most of her holidays traveling to places like Pass Christian, Mississippi. She and her Soup Ladies traveled there cooking for people who were still putting their lives together more than a year after Katrina. She whipped up her famous Stroganoff Soup for a thousand folks at a meal. "Start with 10 pounds of shredded beef and fifteen pounds of sour cream," she says. It turns out that there's always someone in need, so Ginger Passarelli and the Soup Ladies are almost never home for Christmas.

As I remember those radio programs of the 30s, the Cinnamon Bear eventually found the Silver Star, and I suppose I'll find my treasures, too. I only have about fifty boxes left to unpack, so I'm pretty sure to have them by July. Of 2008.

But at least the old house has sold, and though I sure hope you won't mention it to my pastor, I buried a statue of St. Joseph under the "for sale" sign in the front yard. That is supposed to insure the quick sale of your home. When the house is sold, etiquette dictates that you must dig the statue up and put it in a place of honor in your new home. Of course, I understand the mock burial is nothing but silly superstition, but the fact is, the house did sell, and that image of the saint deserves a cushy berth in my new living room. But I'm afraid St. Joseph is stuck in the frozen ground until spring. Sometime in April, I'll ask the new owners if they can spare him. In the meantime, in this season of miracles, may we all find just what we need. Make mine a Silver Star.

Note: Ginger Passarelli and her Soup Ladies continue to make 50 to 60 emergency calls a year to fire and emergency crews bringing comfort and hot soup to the scenes of fires and disasters. They fed crews and displace victims of Hurricane Sandy and the tornadoes in Missouri. "We can be out the door with food for 100 in an hour" The Christian Science Monitor quotes Ginger as saying. Naturally, Ginger and the Soup Ladies were in Oso after the deadly mudslide.

Christmas - 2006

24 Days to Christmas

If you have children, or even grandchildren in your house on a regular basis, there's not much chance that you'll make it all the way to Christmas without going insane. That's a given. You don't even worry about it too much. It's going to happen and that's ok because then you don't have to worry about New Year's Resolutions.

Nothing is more fun than creating unique family holidays. The trick is not to make just one day, December 25, the focus of everything. If you put all the anticipation into that one day, you're bound to be left with an empty feeling when the day is over. If you make every day a celebration, there's more time for religious observance, or time with family and friends, more times to enjoy the wonder for yourself.

Sometimes you really have to reach for the wonder. I once bought my grandson a Polar Express Santa, who said "Believe in the Magic of Christmas" when you pressed his mitten. But the switch to turn him on was in his bottom. It really diminished the effect.

Here are a few ideas that have worked well for me over the years:

1. With the kids grown up and gone, some of us are alone at Christmas more than we'd like to be. Christmas is best shared with others. Recently a group from our Gospel Choir did an impromptu concert at a local hospital for one of our members. It was great fun and rewarding. Why not check around for where you might be needed and do something different.

2. Have a Tradition Party! Choose a family tradition for everyone to learn at this party. We spent one Thanksgiving Day learning to make the traditional fried Italian cookies that, up until then, only my Mom could make. Everyone should take a turn with the dough, the frying, or whatever. Then, the finished product was available for eating or admiring. Sometimes it turns out to be so much trouble you think you should just frame the whole thing.

Someone needs to take the role of narrator and give blow-by-blow instructions into a recorder--or phone--so that everyone has a record of how to accomplish this feat. Be sure to give the little extra tricks.

3. Plan ahead for shopping. For some people, shopping is so much fun that they would feel part of the Christmas celebration was ruined if they didn't get to go out and mix it up at the mall. None of them are me but if you're one who lives to shop, just skip this part. If not, instead of driving yourself crazy running from store to store, do your shopping online. If you don't speak computer, go to the library and go through Christmas catalogs and magazines. Browse through periodicals, and newspapers for great gift ideas. However here's an important note. Do NOT order online from a public computer. Not safe. Transfer ideas to a small notebook which you carry with you all of the time. You can, of course, do it all on your smart phone, except that if you do have a smart phone, it's probably smarter than you are. I know mine is smarter than I am. I say stick to a notebook. Or file cards are good because you can use one card for each person and they're easier to sort. Write down what to buy and for whom. You can eliminate fruitless running around by making some phone calls to be sure the item you want is in stock. Write a "battle plan" of where to go for each gift, grouping errands so that you can shop in several stores in the same area at once. (Allow plenty of time to stop for breaks during the day. Absolutely never go more than two hours without stopping). If you've left all your shopping till the last minute and have to accomplish everything in one massive effort, it can be done. But keep your spirits up by stopping every two hours or so to reward yourself with a beverage break so that you can sit down and relax. Carry a bright-colored envelope and drop all your holiday receipts into it. Then if, Heaven forbid, you must exchange, it will be easier. You're bound to know where that one envelope is. Better yet, write a memoir for your family. Easy to get it printed in a good-looking book format, and your shopping is all done. It's now very easy to put a book together and print it in a very short time.

4. Holiday Baking. Today I met someone who told me that when she was a child, her mother always pointed to a rosy December sunset and

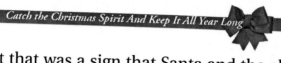

said that that was a sign that Santa and the elves were baking their Christmas cookies. Good for them. And good for you if baking is really fun at your house. Decide whether it's something you want to do. Remember, you can buy cookies and just keep flinging cinnamon on the stove burners when company comes. It will smell like something's cooking and you'll have time for things you really want to do.

5. Family Party--Make memory ornaments. Give everyone a large, plain glass ball (plastic for the kids) and paints or permanent markers. (Get them from Michaels or similar craft store). Everyone can decorate their ornament with some memory of the past year and share the story before they put it on the tree. Everyone can take their own ornaments to their own tree. Or take the lids from coffee cans or disposable refrigerator dishes which make very nice Christmas ornaments. Use your imagination. I remember a retired couple who, one year, decorated their tree with nothing but pictures in plastic frames made from the lids of refrigerator dishes. You always turn out to have more lids than containers which somehow never fit. The dishes are great for shadow boxes.

6. Decorate the family tree. Meaningful for any family get-together. Use a real tree or draw a very big one on poster board. Start with pictures of grandma and grandpa at the top. A different color ribbon for folks from each branch to hang on. Make it more fun by including some family research. Or give a subscription to Ancestry.com for a family gift. It's amazing to actually see where everyone came from. (No, the stork didn't bring you, Johnny). Bring pictures for this year for the bottom branches. It will be fun to see how everyone is interconnected. Be sure you have current pictures and past pictures.

For singles, have everyone bring something special and meaningful to them.

7. Add a little glitz! Easy party decorations: Make full use of mirrors. A mirror tray on the table makes everything look brighter. Put a full-length mirror in the entryway with a Santa Hat and beard fastened on. Everyone can see themselves as Santa. Or find or create a cardboard Santa Family cutout, so everyone can have their picture taken as Santa.

8. Easy sugar plum decorations. Use a piece of styrofoam in tree, bell, or candy cane shape. Decorate with an assortment of gum-drops, mints and life savers, stuck on with either toothpicks, or frosting, if you suspect the elves will be munching.

9. Simplify. Sit down with the family tonight and decide what is really important about the holidays. You may be surprised at the answer. Ask: "What is the one thing that has to happen to make Christmas come for you?" In asking this question of many children, I have been astonished that the answer to that question almost never begins with "presents." When you purchase a gift, make a note of what you bought and where you hid it. Otherwise, Christmas Eve you'll find yourself rushing around with no idea where you put anything.

In a quiet moment, have the family make a wish list with everything they want on it. The wilder the better, and no lectures about being too greedy. This is just for fun, and the sky's the limit. Sit down together and have fun talking the list over, and "what iffing." This is very nearly as much fun as receiving the gifts themselves. If you want, you can have everyone choose the one (reasonable) thing they want. Pick it up and your shopping list is complete and simplified.

10. Cook Just Enough For One Extra Meal and brighten the day for a friend who is alone. People who live alone often just don't bother to cook, but you can add sparkle to someone's day by cooking an extra entree when you make dinner. Freeze and then you can deliver one or a dozen, TV dinner style, labeled with suggestions for companion dishes for a variety of delicious holiday meals. You aren't Meals on Wheels but you can bring a happy day and the fun of an unexpected visit. Be sure the kids go with you to deliver them.

11. Bring the Christmas story to life for your family. Include the grandkids in planning the best way to do this. The neighborhood kids will like it if you have no little ones in your family. If you have a family crèche, set the manger out empty in the place where you want the story to end. If you don't have one, make one from one of those plain papier-mâché boxes you can get at Michaels or other craft shop. Gather the family to-

gether and decide with them where the figures in the Christmas Story belong. Place them throughout the house. Decide on a location for the home of Mary and Joseph. We always liked the dining room for them, for some reason. Perhaps a high bookshelf not too far from "Bethlehem" for the shepherds and sheep, and the wise men might go into the back bedrooms. Be careful to note where you put them, we lost one of our wise men for two years. Well, we didn't exactly lose him, but he disappeared and a couple of Christmases later, he turned up in the china cabinet with, I would swear, a happy smile on his face. Let family members take turns moving the figures closer day by day, and as you move them, talk about how the people involved felt, the significance of what happened on the Christmas journey and how we can reflect it in our own lives. One way we chose to do this in our family was to have a small bag of straw near the manger. Whenever any member of the family does a "good deed" or has a special reason to feel joy, that person has the fun of adding straw to the manger to prepare a soft bed for the Holy Infant when He comes. To make this really work, Mom and Dad should join in the activity. The kids may surprise you with their interpretation. I remember my daughter coming to me after she judged that her brother had been especially obnoxious and demanding, "Make him take five straws OUT." On Christmas Eve, you may choose to conclude the ceremony by having a family procession.

In our home, the holy family "arrive" at their destination early in the day. Late on Christmas Eve, even at midnight as the children grew older, there was a procession, with carol singing and usually, it was the privilege of the youngest child present to put the Baby Jesus in the manger. These are followed by children and guests carrying the shepherds and sheep. Award the donkey with discretion. Some people take offense at having custody of the ass. It has been our custom to wait until January 5th to add the wise men. But every family should establish their own traditions. After all, this story belongs to every one of us and will work best if the personal heritage is included. You can't go wrong getting the kids' advice and direction.

12. Make the season more fun and less hectic by celebrating the special days within the season. For instance, December 6th is St Nicholas Day, a great day for making specially decorated Santa Claus cookies to share with the neighborhood kids. St. Lucy's Day is December 10. It's the festival of lights. You might do something as simple a decorating the table with extra candles. For years our eldest daughter woke her father and me on St. Lucy's day with a song and fresh coffee cake, because we had convinced her that this was how the day was properly celebrated. Then she found out that none of the other kids in her class had to do it, and she promptly turned in her resignation.

December 13 is the Feast of Our Lady of Guadalupe. Have a dinner of Mexican Food and finish off the event with a piñata. Kids love nothing as much as something to destroy. No kids in your house? Make one for you and your friends to destroy. You'll be amazed at how much fun it is to beat something to smithereens. There are many reasons to celebrate. Why not create your own. Nothing is more fun than unique family holidays.

13. But what if you are alone? A listener

called to say, "Those ideas are very nice, but what if you don't have a family to move the nativity set around with?" In that event, try this. Make yourself a gift of love. You do it this way:

Find a sturdy box. Wrap it in Christmas paper. Make it pretty. Cut a slit in the top just like a Valentine box. Beside it, place a pencil and some slips of paper. Every time you see evidence of the Christmas spirit around you - you read something or hear something that speaks to your heart. Or a friend does something special. Even a TV program that makes you laugh. Clip it out, or write it down and put it in the box. Whenever you feel down, or sorry for yourself, reach in and pull out just a slip or two and read it. We do all receive many gifts every day, but often we allow them to pass unnoticed. On Christmas Eve or Christmas Day, settle down and give yourself plenty of time to enjoy everything in the box. See how rich you really are.

24. Plan a special day just for you. Especially if you are alone, pick up the calendar right now and circle a date - one or better two or three that will be for you alone. Call a friend and arrange a luncheon or a shopping trip. Dress up, go to a nice restaurant, and spend some time choosing or buying a gift for yourself that you ordinarily would consider just a bit extravagant. My first Christmas alone after my husband died, I realized that there would not be the special gift that my husband had usually chosen. It may seem trivial, but it was one thing more than I could bear. I went through the catalog just like the kids, circled a few things I really wanted, and gave them permission to use my credit card to buy a gift which would represent the love we shared. The children made the selections and wrapped the gifts and I had my usual mysterious packages to poke and feel and rattle. I don't have to do that now, of course, but it helped that first Christmas. If you are living through transition, look at the things that are really important to you, and begin now planning strategies to help adjust. No matter how silly they might seem to someone else, if they help you, do it! Give yourself permission to enjoy something special. But remember that almost always, it's going to be reaching out to someone else that will bring the most joy. I know that sounds terribly like a Hallmark Holiday Movie, but it's true.

25. String a Danish "Treat Line" Here's a unique family custom that's shared by a Danish family. String a rope across the dining room wall from which hang all sorts of goodies, like popcorn balls, gingerbread men, fruit and little boxes filled with fudge and candy. Each gift is numbered. Place a duplicate set of numbers in a paper bag. Starting with the youngest child, everyone picks a number and takes a corresponding gift. Keep drawing until all are gone. Divide and munch leftovers. A good way to give small gifts to kids and unexpected drop-ins, too.

Create some special family activities. Get a full-size piece of foam core board (or even cardboard will work well) and let each family member draw their home, decorate, add distinguishing features, and a road linking it with the rest of the board. Make historical notes. *The Wilhelms came to Monroe and opened the town grocery store in 1899. Youngsters can use miniature cars to drive from one place to the other. Pick up miniatures in second hand stores from time to time. The kids will spend hours and days driving the

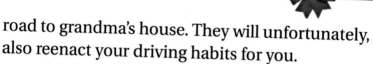

road to grandma's house. They will unfortunately, also reenact your driving habits for you.

We have a compromise. My Christmas cookies are Christmas colored M&M's substituted for Chocolate chips in a regular cookie recipe. Bakes in minutes. If you keep a roll of cookie dough in the freezer, you can turn out fresh cookies in minutes when friends arrive.

Don't pass up any opportunities for fun. At a gift shop yesterday, I watched as a man who appeared to be in his sixties flitted around the store, turning on all of the electronic Christmas figures as the sales people watched aghast. Soon, forty seven jolly Santas and elves were singing Jingle Bells. At slightly different intervals. The vibrations from all those jingles caused the Santas to bounce to the edge of their tables and slowly slide onto the floor. At last, I saw something I could do. "You stand right there" I told him in my most reproving mother voice, "till every last one of these things stops jingling and catch them." The miscreant froze and stood by the table meekly, clutching the edge of two Santa's robes. His wife came to find him and he said, "She said I have to stay here, "looking at me fearfully." I felt great. That felt really good. That was a step in the right direction. Catch the Christmas Spirit when you can and keep it all year long.

Merry Christmas!

Celebrating!

I found an embroidered cushion in a box which contained some of my late Aunt Vi's treasures. It was right next to her belly dancing costume, and the silver studded black leather wrestling belt. Vi was a professional wrestler, you may remember, but it looks as if she may have stitched this pillow herself. Vi always had a bit of an attitude. So does this motto which features a blunt Anglo Saxon expression that translates for this family newspaper as "To heck with the golden years." There are days when that sentiment seems very appropriate.

The years past the age of forty can be rewarding; that's been well documented. It seems that every day a different author releases a book which explores the many joys of being fifty. Then we get to the years after sixty and the cheering section falls strangely silent. There's just the hint of a cold wind at the back of the neck. It's hard to pinpoint what has changed, but I've noticed a few indicators. For instance, I still have my photographic memory, only now the film is overexposed. The other night I was actually turned down by a singles agency which was making a cold call. "Oh, we can't take women over 55," the caller caroled. "There are just not enough men interested in women that age." And she'd called me. Thanks.

Those of us enjoying these golden years are definitely not wimps. We are mountain climbers; we are skiers; we leave perfectly serviceable airplanes to skydive.

Nothing is beyond our reach. I have a friend who's nearly seventy. She works out three times a week. She is pumping iron. She spends hours on the stair climber and the stationary bike. I admire that. I don't do it, but I surely do admire it.

I have to admit that I'm having just a little trouble getting motivated. I don't pump iron, unless you count lifting a soup can from cupboard to stove. In this beautiful weather, the neighbors are all out walking. I don't do that either. I started to take dancing lessons but then I injured a groin muscle and had to quit. It wasn't even my groin muscle but they made me quit anyway.

My world is changing fast. Every mail delivery brings an announcement or an invitation with the astounding news that some child who was barely in pigtails a week ago, in Pampers last month, is graduating from high school or college or, heaven help us, getting married.

I went to a wedding last weekend. It was the first marriage for the happy couple - noteworthy in these days. She at 34 and he at 47 were, as the bride told me, old enough to appreciate each other. They glowed with happiness and when they were pronounced man and wife, the bride actually gave a small leap of joy, to the delighted applause of assembled friends.

Moments like that are rare gifts and they're gifts I treasure. But I'm going to level with you. Moments like that are also getting just a just a little tough to handle. They make it harder to go home alone. I can only spend so much time on the tasteful presentation of my Yorkie, Bibi's can of Gourmet Dog Entrees, even though nothing is too good for my best friend.

Years ago, when I was struggling with cancer, a friend brought me a pretty container. It was an empty shoe box, wrapped in fabric, with a slit cut in the top like a valentine holder. "For you, to catch the good things that happen" she said. "Don't let good times get away. Write down everything good that happens, and collect the memories in this box. I'll be back to check on you," she said sternly. That's good advice that I try to follow whenever the house gets too quiet.

I look for moments to celebrate. When someone asks, "How are you?" I focus on a positive event and I answer, "Celebrating, thank you." For example, an e-mail brings the news that my granddaughter has won two races in her swimming competitions. "Celebrating, thank you."

There's a message from my grandson who invites me to come watch him play in a baseball game. Only, he reminds, last time I went to a game he broke his arm. He hopes that isn't a trend. "Celebrating, thank you."

Turns out you can celebrate getting together with a friend to make chocolate dipped strawberries, or finding a book on tape that brightens hours in the car, or a rose that unaccountably blooms when I'd given up hope.

"Celebrating, thank you."

Every season is the season of gifts.

How am I? Celebrating, thank you. How are you?

Spring – 1995

Note: In this column, I made quite a point of not exercising. Not too long after that, my doctor informed me that starting immediately, I would be walking at least one half hour a day. "I don't have to do that," I blustered. "No," he replied, "and I don't have to take care of you." So now I walk two miles a day, and take Tai Chi three times a week, so I do have to take back what I said about exercise.

My Stars!

The announcement came in the mail yesterday. A star in the cosmos has been named for me. It's about time. The presentation folder, suitable for framing, or at least for waving around ostentatiously, lists the coordinates and says that my star is in the constellation Leo Minor. This unexpected honor is a birthday gift from two of my sons who, in a flight of fancy impossible to justify, have designated the star as Dorothy's Eternal Flame.

"You are not easy to choose presents for," Son Patrick explains. "All your children agree on that." Naturally, I am delighted that all my children have talked to each other long enough to agree on this, or anything for that matter. And it could be true that their complaints are justified. I've got to admit I had been dreading this birthday. But, heck, I dread every birthday. This is a lifelong pattern for me. I took to my bed for three days on either side of my 29th birthday while the whole family tiptoed in and out, looking puzzled.

Family legend says that on my 37th birthday, I experienced meltdown upon catching sight of the candles on the cake. This year I started in early December looking forward to the big day with dread. Do your birthday sniveling early, is my motto.

Living up to my expectations, this birthday got off to an inauspicious start. First I made the mistake of dressing without turning the light on. It's amazing that things that look perfectly good in the dark can look really bad as soon as you can see them. Did you ever notice how hard it is to feel alluring when you're wearing one black shoe and one brown one? Also, in the dark, you can't see the tomato dribbles on your blouse. They show up nicely just as soon as you get to wherever a large crowd of people is gathered, though.

Next, I took the wrong exit off the freeway and ended up at the entrance to Fort Lewis. The guard at the gate of this Army installation was pleasant, helpful, and very, very military. He gave me directions to my destination and then, while I was still making notes, whipped out a razor blade and scraped the military sticker off the car. "Expired," he explained tersely. I think he was speaking about the tags and not me. I'm not sure, though.

There's no use fretting. It just eats up brain cells, but it's hard not to get spun up in questions like "will the additives in my food cause me to grow hair on my upper lip?" If not, what is doing it?

All of this made me look toward the future with a jaundiced eye. If this was the beginning, the prospects for the year ahead seemed pretty dismal. "I've had a lot of trouble in my life, most of which never happened," Mark twain said. Me, too. Dreading what was ahead, I forgot the birthday gift you have to give yourself: the ability to appreciate each day. Just be fully there today. Every day. There's nothing like a star to bring you down to earth.

So let me be the first to admit that my attitude toward birthdays is totally unjustified. After all, many cultures completely ignore adult birthdays. I am definitely not alone with this problem. Neither are you. According to the Assistant Secretary for Aging (yes, there really is one) 5,190 of us turn 66 every single day. If that doesn't cheer you up, I hesitate to imagine what might do it.

People over fifty are just getting their second wind. The new attitude is definitely energetic. Folks in their 70's are celebrating festive occasions on skis, hogs (the two wheeled kind), and roller blades. You've got to be in pretty good shape to age gracefully in this new millennium.

Now, of course, a star certificate is just a novelty gift and the folks at International Star Registry are the first to admit it. The true naming of a star is restricted to a very few members of the international scientific community, and isn't a privilege that's for sale. Still, in the past twenty years 500,000 stars have been registered in the name of people like Frank Sinatra, Madonna, Elvis Presley - and me. Right this minute, Dorothy's Eternal Flame is up there blinking away – somewhere. That makes me smile.

You and I both know that the real "star moments" can't be bought or sold. They come when you get an unexpected call from a granddaughter or a spontaneous hug from a teenage grandson. A star moment comes when a daughter in law asks for advice - and takes it. These are the things that really make the stars come out.

It turns out that anyone can have a star named for her but no one can own a star. They're there for all of us to reach toward. That's a very good thing, too.

New Year - 2000

Irresolute

I have just passed that birthday in which the government takes undue interest. In the daily mail, I receive stacks of brochures from people who seem to believe that the high point of my life from now on is going to be choosing the right nursing home or cemetery plot. I can hardly wait. I don't mind admitting that I could use a little insight into the years ahead but there isn't much available. Books and articles abound touting the wonders of life at fifty. Well, let me tell you something: Fifty is for sissies! For wimps! It's when you pass sixty, when you need help most, that the experts fall strangely silent. This, my friends, is where the rubber meets the road. Let's at least make a start. I am proud to step forward to represent my generation with these thought provoking observations about life in the semi-fast lane after sixty.

1) It takes a lot longer to wake up in the morning. You lie in bed and wonder. What day is

this? What year is this? What town is this? What's my name? Who cares? If you can roll over, the best thing to do is go back to sleep. If not, proceed to paragraph two.

2) You notice signs of aging in pets and friends. The dog and I are going downhill together. We both have arthritis and a thyroid condition. Every morning we get up and make our way stiffly toward the back door so Bibi can get out to commune with nature. She communes on a more regular basis than I. We are a bit stiffer every day. I just hope no one is planning to have either one of us put to sleep.

3) Personal great expectations become slightly diminished. The kids at the studio gave me a copy of Love and Sex After Sixty. The pages were blank.

4) Expect to spend more time comparing pains. I used to wonder why people indulged in such dull stuff. Turns out, it's like a reverse adolescence where you struggle to understand the new rules of the game. Last week I sampled a trial membership with an over fifty singles computer matching group. One correspondent wrote that

he enjoys "making love by a tumbling stream." Then he spent the rest of his letter discussing his degenerative knee condition, so my understanding was that if we found that tumbling stream, the damp wasn't going to do his joints much good. Cancel my subscription.

5) Everything starts to look just a little blurry but you still won't wear glasses. The exception is thirty seconds at the start of any gathering when glasses may be donned briefly for a quick glance over the crowd. Then you say, "O.K. I've seen everyone." and whisk the glasses off. Anyone who wasn't there for the official scan won't be recognized the rest of the evening. Sometimes that 's better. I have a friend who found her new glasses enchanting. She saw her grandchildren clearly for the first time and was astonished. "I always thought they had such dull, plain little faces," she confessed. She was also surprised at television. She had thought she wasn't watching TV because she couldn't see it clearly. Now with her new glasses she can clearly see that there's nothing to watch. That's progress!

6) You can't take medicine that comes in

child proof containers, unless you can get your grandchildren to come open them for you. Children under five can conquer them easily.

In short, life has suddenly become much more complicated than I expected and requires my concentrated attention. In other years by this time, I would have already made and broken all of my New Year's resolutions but I don't make resolutions anymore.

My mother believed that a successful year must start with firm resolve. We sat around those cold dark Montana nights in the late 30's with the snow falling outside, listening to the Mercury Radio Theater and the stove popping while we worked over our lists of character improving, specific plans for the next year. Maybe, on second thought I will make one resolution this year.

I do resolve to enjoy every day; to see people I really want to see. I can entertain up to six people at a time. I have that many matching saucers left from my Spencerian Rose trousseau china. My son offered to buy me a new set of dishes. Why would I want that? Six is a perfect number of people for an interesting evening. We must make our own fun. If the tumbling stream makes your knees hurt, go somewhere dry. Let's not miss a minute. I was recently given a cell phone. It is an ideal size for me; big enough for the numbers to be legible and small enough to fit in my purse without making me walk funny. Now you can call me anywhere. My purse will ring, and I will answer it--unless I've turned off the phone to enjoy a quiet moment with a grandchild or watch a sunset or take a nap. Are we having fun yet? The party starts just as soon as I answer my purse.

New Year - 1997

Party On!

It is terrible to have a birthday at the beginning of the year. I guarantee you can't raise any interest in a party of any sort. No birthday should be allowed until there has been time for making preparations, making mistakes, having a face lift. If I knew where to complain I would demand an adjustment. I won't tell you which birthday it is, but I will say I've received a letter from the Social Security Administration expressing unusual interest. In the same mail came my annual letter from the Department of the Army, requesting reassurance that I haven't somehow managed to get married during the past year. No way, fellows.

I have never been good at birthdays. There's something about the idea of aging gracefully that annoys heck out of me. The trouble with birthdays is that they seem to bring multiple obligations as you get older. In early adulthood, you just have birthdays. Go out to dinner. Have a beer or two. Say good night. Now Medicaid is waiting in the wings. I get daily entreaties to consider a variety of medical plans allegedly created specifically with my personal best interests at heart. I am flattered. Each brochure details overall altruism and so much general goodwill toward personkind that it's apparent each and every company is vying to be named as Mother Teresa's successor. Hard choices.

Now the custom is to put one candle on the cake and head for the hills, leaving me to assess the damage myself.

I'm not sure that 1998 shows particular promise. My mother used to invite each new year into her home by standing on the front porch striking my grandmother's tambourine against one hip while pounding on a dishpan with an antique soup ladle. It was a pretty impressive display. It worked fine when she lived in rural Montana, but the neighbors weren't wild about it when we moved to the city. My daughter has modified this practice and prefers to welcome the new year by playing her university fight song. There's something soul-stirring about hearing "Mighty Oregon" on the tuba in the middle of the night. I probably shouldn't have mentioned this. Up until now, the neighbors may not have been exactly sure where the unexpected serenades originated.

I always use the arrival of the new year for the annual ceremonial cleaning out my purse. My purse weighs 13.8 pounds. That's roughly the size of a large roast or a small dog. It contains everything I need to sustain life for twenty-four hours. It has been registered with the Bureau of Weights and Measures, the Directory of National Monuments and the Immigration and Naturalization Service. It has been said that my handbag contains one of everything that has been made since the beginning of time, but that is not strictly true. It does make me walk funny.

In his book, *Where To Go From Here*, gerontologist James E. Birren suggests that we review our past in order to define our future. Ask meaningful questions, he urges. Ask yourself, "What are some of the good times I've enjoyed? How do I make good times happen now?" Start small. For instance, this might be a good day to send out my Christmas cards. Friends won't be sure whether they're early for '98 or late for '97. I'm not sure, either. Good times are where you find them.

This will be a year of surprises. There are already some intriguing signs. The new copy of *The Yearbook of Experts, Authorities and Spokespersons* for 1998 has arrived. It lists Dorothy Wilhelm--yes, this Dorothy Wilhelm--as an expert on "Sex after Fifty." There it is on page 159, right after "Sex Addiction" and right before "Sex and Love." I couldn't be more astonished. I sort of rubbed at the print on the page but it doesn't come off. To tell the truth, I don't know whether to demand an apology and a correction, or to keep quiet on the theory that perhaps they know something I don't. And I really don't. I did get a call from a radio station in Las Vegas which asked some very thought-provoking questions. Perhaps sometime during the year ahead I'll arrive at the answers.

New Year - 1998

iPod Birthday

My children, apparently under the impression that I am someone else altogether, gave me an iPod for my birthday. There's no instruction manual. "It's very intuitive," my son explained.

For those still living in the technological dark ages, which is where I spend a lot of time, an iPod downloads favorite sound, music and video from your computer. That allows you to enjoy your own carefully chosen selections constantly while pretty much ignoring everyone else. Very desirable. Mine came with a digital speaker system with crystal clear sound, which means that you will be enjoying my personal music too.

My computer seemed curiously reluctant to enter into this adventure with me, but after numerous telephone consultations with tech support I was able to plug the iPod into my USB port. (Let's see the hands of those who didn't even know their computer had a USB port. Ha! I thought so). I can recognize the USB because it has a little twisty icon that looks sort of like a cactus or a dead tree.

Oh joy! Immediately, the high visibility two inch screen lit up with my first message. I leaned forward excitedly to squint at the teeny tiny letters. It said, translated from tech talk, "Your computer cannot connect to this iPod with its gloriously crystal clear screen, designed in Cupertino California and assembled in China, because you have an operating system that slightly predates the founding of the Roman Empire."

"You're going to need to update the system," the support tech explained. "You're certainly going to need more memory." Apparently, you get memory on a card and you can stick it where you need it. No rude comments, please. They tell me this tiny electronic wafer, only about two by four inches, has more memory than the hard disk on my computer. I'm not surprised, because my computer doesn't remember a lot more than I do. And I don't remember much.

Recently, a friend gave me a pin with my name spelled out in letters two inches high, so that if I should, in a moment of excitement, forget who or where I am I can just glance down surrep-

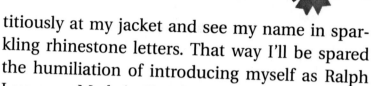

titiously at my jacket and see my name in sparkling rhinestone letters. That way I'll be spared the humiliation of introducing myself as Ralph Lauren or Made in Singapore.

It's fair to say that technological comprehension hasn't often come easily. The last time I was on the cutting edge of technology was when I was fourteen and my father gave me one of the very first portable tape recorders. It had miniature three-inch reels in a spiffy red plastic case, and I was the hit of every party for about three months. Then Judie Crawford got one, and that was the end of that.

Still, I know I can get this to work. I'm a 21st Century woman, after all. A recent survey by U.S. health care coordinator Evercare says that of 100 people aged 99 years and older, they found that four percent of respondents had listened to music on an iPod. It doesn't say what the other 96% of people were doing, but clearly that four percent has kids that just won't give up.

My line of computers names its operating systems after jungle cats like "Panther" or "Jaguar" to appear more jaunty and exciting. I think my current system is called "Dysfunctional Tom Cat." Anyway, to use my birthday prize, I need to upgrade to "Leopard." This may be very hard to manage when my Home Owners Association doesn't even want me to have a dog, but I have confidence that soon I'll be bouncing along to my own interior music--and for once, it won't be created by the sounds of my digestive tract.

In the meantime after several tries, the computer still isn't a "Leopard" and my iPod remains tauntingly silent, waiting for one of the computer techie kids to come to the rescue. At times like this, it's comforting to fall back on some familiar low-tech favorites. Among my birthday gifts were six pair of socks. Assorted colors. No batteries required and no instructions needed. My feet are nice and warm, but for now the music stays in my heart.

Note: This is one of the few columns where readers' reaction was uniformly negative. I was roundly scolded for completely overlooking the fact that my children had gone to a lot of trouble and expense to plan a special gift for me and all I did was make fun of it. One reader said she'd never read anything I write again. Although it's late, I want to apologize to readers and my children for underappreciating a perfect gift that has provided me with hours of joy. DJW

New Year - 2008

Easter! Stash the Trash

I can't believe it's already March. I just hope I can get the Christmas decorations out of sight before Easter. I admit I haven't exactly rushed to put them away this year, because to tell the truth, I'm not sure I'll be able to find them again.

I know there are people who have all of their seasonal decorations filed in color-coded boxes and wrapped in acid-free paper. They even have each item inventoried in perfect order to be located at a moment's notice. Easter in, Christmas out, and they're not even breathing hard. There are such people, some in my own family. I am not one of them. I am one of those folks who somehow can never quite get it together--and if we did get it together, we wouldn't have any idea where we'd put it.

I have every birthday card I ever received in a towering stack on my desk. I am convinced that if I move the pile, I will never find any single item again. Experience bears this out. Over the course of time, I have said a premature goodbye to my military ID, several airline tickets, my daughter's vaccination certificate and my homeowner's insurance policy, and that was in a relatively good week. I also misplaced the iron, (for clothes, not curling) though I never really missed it, and lost the dog in a downstairs bedroom for two days, but that's another story.

My trouble is that I can't throw anything away. You never know when you might need it. Well, yes, you do know. You'll need it within 24 hours after the garbage truck hauls it away. At least twice a month one or another of my children turns in the direction of an undefined pile of debris and remarks in a carefully conversational tone that, after nearly thirty years in the same house, I will certainly be more comfortable when I "downsize and consolidate some of this mess, in case you need to move to a smaller home." That's ridiculous. I need more room, not less. If I move, it will be to somewhere l like--Cheney Stadium or the deck of the Titanic. I am making progress, though. This year for the first time, I single-handedly cut the discarded Christmas tree into four-foot segments so it could go into the recycling bin. Of course that was only last week, but still, progress is progress.

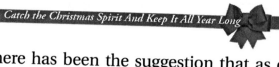

There has been the suggestion that as one ages, it is simply harder to let go of things. Nonsense. I know that each cherished item will prove vital one of these days. Think of it as the ultimate in recycling. For instance, even leftover fabric softener sheets are valuable. Stick 'em in the grandkids' sneakers to render them (the shoes, not the kids) socially acceptable. Always carry a fabric softener sheet in the car. If you get out of the car with static cling and your skirt clinging to every lumpy inch of your anatomy, you subtly run the sheet under your skirt or trouser legs and the cling lets go like magic. Of course, everyone will wonder what on earth you're doing. Make up your own excuse. I can't solve every little problem for you.

I have a friend who simply tacks important papers on the wall. The wall looks awful, but he absolutely never loses anything. Another acquaintance crosses her fingers when she has something to remember for a short time. That works fine; keeps the fingers supple. If she has two things to remember, she crosses fingers on both hands and that works. Three things is okay. But if she has to remember any more, she can't pick anything up.

The bathroom mirror is my location of choice for posting reminders about things that need to be done. This provides an extra incentive, because if I leave too much undone I can't see to put on my makeup.

This morning I received an email from a journalist asking me to comment on a story about an 82-year-old man who continues to pursue his career as a professional nude artist's model. What can I say? As a person who has frequently been asked to keep her clothes on, I am filled with awe. This certainly provides inspiration. After all, this gentleman is obviously improving his skills, learning something new every day. If he can do it, we all can. I can learn new habits. I can make changes. I can get those decorations into their boxes.

But, wait, what's the hurry after all? I am not personally bothered by the sight of my collection of Santas jockeying for space on the mantel with the Easter bunnies. In fact, why not just give Santa an Easter Basket and let him join the springtime crowd? We all have to accept where we are, and it's time the jolly old elf learned a few new job skills.

Easter - 1998

Father's Day

The boy who would grow up to be my father was a gangling 12-year-old, already over six feet tall, when he decided to enlist in the Marines in 1919. And he got away with it. The war was over, but the glamour of military service remained. "Nothing to it," said my father, talking about the adventure years later.

"I just wrote the number 18 on a piece of paper, stuck it in my shoe, and said, "I'm over 18." That way it was a true statement, depending how you looked at it. He described the recruiting poster that captured him. While the other services used slick placards like James Montgomery Flagg's iconic "Uncle Sam wants you," the Marine poster was different. It was a scrap of torn brown paper stuck on the post office wall. Eight words were scrawled across it. "You're not good enough to be a Marine," it said. That sold him.

Miraculously, the boy made it through basic training--boot camp--before his parents tracked him down. He refused to go home with them, promised to run away again, but his folks took him back to West Virginia. True to his word, young Joe kept running away. He traveled to most of the 48 states, changing his name as often as his location, and after awhile his folks gave up. He worked in the Oklahoma oil fields, and he spent time as a cowboy in Texas. It was nothing like a John Wayne movie. "It ain't pretty," he drawled.

I remember him as a tough father, setting standards impossible for a five year old to meet. I adored him, but I was always a little afraid of him. When I was married, he didn't speak to me or my new husband for a year. I had taken the unpardonable step of marrying a career Army officer and a Catholic. If you couldn't marry a Marine, why bother! Worse yet, I had married just after Christmas, depriving him of his deserved tax deduction, even though I'd lived under his roof the whole year.

But something magic happens when a boy becomes a grandfather. And it happened for my Dad. Overnight, he became "Grandpappy," endlessly patient, loving, and funny. Down on the floor on all fours, letting little ones crawl up his sides and swing from his arms, singing songs, using comic voices to tell the "real "story of the Three Little Pigs and Goldilocks. He'd sit for hours with a fretful three-year-old, carefully popping single morsels of cereal into the tiny questing mouth. He became a family legend, as all good Grandfathers do.

I see the same change in my sons. Hard to believe that the same little fellow who used to store dried worms in his pockets is now a grandfather, tenderly cuddling the small boys who will, no doubt, be fathers, too, one day. So it was in this sentimental mood last week that I packed a bulgy suitcase with gifts and headed to Minnesota for a visit with the youngest grandchildren. I took a talking fly swatter for my son. It came in a very nice gift box. The fly swatter says such things as "Gotcha!" or "Hasta la Vista!" as you swat the fly. I don't know why you couldn't say these things yourself and save money, but I saw some really big flies in Minnesota so perhaps it's best to conserve your energy for the actual swat.

My signature activity on these visits is

making animal-shaped pancakes. We made elephants and camels and rabbits. Anything you can't identify is either a whale or an amoeba. Or a rattlesnake. "My Daddy knows how to make real pancakes," my youngest Grandson observed. It turns out that real pancakes are frozen and come in a box from the supermarket with big red letters. Who knew?

A high point of the visit was when we watched Older Grandson star as King Solomon in a church play. "Couldn't we just do a DNA test?" the King asked plaintively when the two mothers brought their "sniffly, snuffly baby who cries all the time" to him for his wise decision. We were all proud when he decided the right way, and we clapped and laughed a lot the way grandparents do at church plays.

Afterward, back at his house, our four-year-old basked in the afterglow of his exemplary rendition of "Twinkle, Twinkle." He leaned comfortably back into his father's arms and remarked to me, "Your little kid turned out to be my Daddy." Magic, isn't it?

Fathers Day - 2010

Do You Believe We Did That?

The first bottle of root beer exploded at just about ten o'clock in the morning on the Fourth of July. As usual. You need those time-honored traditions to get your holiday off to the right start. Our tradition was that my mother always made root beer for the Fourth of July and it always exploded. I won't say that Independence Day was better when I was a child, but it certainly was more interesting.

Soft drinks didn't come in cans in those days. If you wanted root beer, you had to go to a soda fountain in some big town like Libby or you had to make it yourself. We'd all seen pictures of Santa Claus holding a bottle of his preferred soft drink, but he'd certainly never bought any to Warland, Montana. It was pretty generally agreed that a proper Independence Day celebration required root beer and Old Man Dean (As far as I know, his mother named him "Old Man," for he was always called by that name) did the honors for many uneventful years, until the Game Warden invited him to the Lincoln County seat for an extended stay. My mother volunteered bravely to take over the chore. I have no idea why. The first year her brew was perfect. That really was unfortunate, because that convinced Mother that she was a gifted brewer of root beer, and every year after that, she brewed root beer and every year it exploded.

Root beer really shouldn›t be that hard to brew, at least theoretically. Flavoring, sugar and water are all you need, according to www.hoptech.com. The problem is the fizziness. If you don't put in enough ale yeast, the drink is flat; too much, and you have shrapnel flying all over the yard.

After the explosions stopped and the glass was raked to the side of the yard for another year, we all walked down the road to taste Betty Evans's new batch of traditional 4th of July pickles. They were just terrible as always, tasting strongly of kerosene. "Don't you say anything bad about Mrs. Evans' pickles," hissed my mother, putting her patented pinch/grab hold on my shoulder.

"It's an old family recipe," Betty Evans said with satisfaction. Apparently it was acquired from a family member who was not wholly friendly. I really could have used the root beer to wash it down.

We had no way of knowing that would be our last Fourth of July there by the Kootenai River. World War II started that winter and the whole town moved to Spokane for defense work, and Santa started taking his bottled soft drinks to the troops overseas. Now that I'm grown up, of course, I endorse the idea of Safe and Sane celebrations.

Looking back though, it seems that always, in those years and after, our best celebrations always were those tinged with humor and maybe a bit of danger where you shake your head and say, "Can you BELIEVE we did that?"

For instance, when the Coast Guard Barque *Eagle* visited for the Tall Ships celebration, I couldn't help remembering another Fourth of July when my son sailed on *Eagle*. I dampened his celebration considerably by actually calling the Admiral to complain that my son wasn't writing to me often enough. Can you BELIEVE I did that?

He sure started writing, though.

A close friend, celebrating her recovery from heart surgery as she rounds the corner toward 80, treated herself to the Girls' Schwinn bike she never had as a child. "I can't BELIEVE you did that," I said.

"It sure is fun," she says, as she rides around the neighborhood.

Yes, she has a safety helmet. Our celebrations don't have to be wrapped in plastic, and they should reflect who we are right now.

Here in Pleasantville we had our usual picture-perfect Fourth of July. The food was perfect, the pickles were crisp without a hint of kerosene and nothing exploded. Nothing at all. I can't BELIEVE we did that. I think I'll just look around and see if I can't find that old root beer recipe.

Fourth of July - 2010

SQUAWK!

Just as I pulled the huge Thanksgiving turkey from the oven, golden brown and roasted to perfection, it began to squawk. I'm not meaning some wimpy little noise caused by sizzling grease. No. I'm talking about loud, strident cries. This was decidedly unsettling. It seems that somehow air had been trapped in the great bird's breast and neck area as it cooked, causing it to emit a strident and insistent squawk whenever you touched it, as if it was protesting its sad condition. It was heart wrenching, all right, but we ate it anyway. When you have a hungry crowd in the house, you certainly can't retreat to canned tuna. Martha Stewart does not cover this in any of her books, I might point out.

There's no denying that some pretty alarming things have come out of my oven over the years, and I'm not even counting the drying tennis shoes and papier-mâché puppet heads. I'm talking about actual food.

For instance, there was the year of the exploding squash. In my opinion, squash should come with a warning label. "Danger! Explosive! Run for your life!" Something subtle and understated like that. The year I learned about the unstable qualities of this vegetable was the year we decided to have baked squash instead of candied sweet potatoes for Thanksgiving dinner. It was also the year I learned a valuable life lesson. I hate when that happens. You'll find it hard to believe, but I hadn't realized that if you don't cut a squash into pieces or at the least poke holes in it, that humble vegetable can achieve basically the same thrust as an Apollo space ship when it is cooked, and will self-launch. So as the squash came out of the oven, it exploded. Pieces rocketed to the ceiling. Other fragments ricocheted around the kitchen like shrapnel, and still others struck my arms or stuck on the front of my glasses (which at least protected my eyes). As the molten squash cooled, it left indelible spots on my kitchen ceiling and a scar shaped like a T-bone steak on my arm. That one's not in *The New Joy of Cooking*, either. I'll certainly never underestimate a squash again.

All of these experiences were very much on my mind last week when I went to check out a new condominium community for people past 55. My children are anxious for me to find a smaller home. "Get out of that big, ugly old thing, Mother," they say of the house where I've lived for thirty years. This development featured attractive individual homes with postage stamp lawns which someone else would manicure. I walked around the perfect kitchen. The salesman, 21 and just out of college, extolled the value of living in a community where there would be only people my own age. No little children running around. "I don't think I like the idea of just people my age," I said. It has always seemed to me that we'd get dull if we associate only with people like ourselves. The salesman looked surprised--and a bit disdainful. "Well then, all you'd have is a neighborhood," he said.

I spent a long time looking into the oven. It was very clean and shiny. Not like my old model which always looks like it had recently hosted The Battle of Britain. I'll bet the permanently blackened interior of my old oven is responsible for the fact that I perpetually turn out lopsided cakes which have about as many dips and holes as the average golf course.

I learned to overcome the problem of the cakes by stuffing the misshapen areas between just the unfrosted layers of special occasion cakes with marshmallows, held in place with chocolate kisses turned over and pushed into the cake like thumbtacks. This useful trick allows you to create a level surface, and once the cake is frosted it looks perfect. The chocolate and marshmallow melt together and make a nice surprise when you bite into the cake. I baked those lopsided cakes for years and my kids either didn't notice, or thought I did it on purpose. Although when my sons married girls who effortlessly baked light fluffy desserts which needed no extra support, one of the boys did question why his birthday cake no longer had "all the good stuff inside."

So in that shining model home, I stood a long time peering into the oven. It had easy to read dials and lights. I'm sure any cake to come out of its space age interior would be perfect. It's just that I'm not sure I'm ready for perfection. What if I can't do without those special cakes, with their magical filling of marshmallows and chocolates--and love? Until I can answer that question, I'm not moving anywhere. That old oven may have its faults, but it can go on as it is awhile longer. So can I.

Thanksgiving - 1997

Real Holidays and Fake Ones

I love holidays. I always have. I celebrate the real holidays and the fake ones. I've just bought a case of chunky peanut butter to celebrate National Peanut Butter Lovers' Month in November. There just can't be enough holidays for me.

I used to start months ahead and work long hours each day to make each family holiday--birthdays, Thanksgiving and Christmas--absolutely perfect. I started buying magazines in summer, tested ideas and planned each detail. The Thanksgiving table had to be perfectly set with handmade pinecone turkey favors. One Christmas we made napkin rings from toilet paper rolls (empty) topped with felt poinsettias. I don't remember exactly why we did that, but I do know that was the last toilet paper roll craft I ever care to make. Another year, I sprayed everything including the front of the refrigerator with gold spray paint. The children made cereal mosaics which I also sprayed gold. Note: It doesn't work to spray Cheerios gold.

They sort of collapse. Then the kids cry and you'll sort of collapse. I often worked late into the night right up to Christmas Eve to have everything ready down to the perfect dusting of talcum powder Santa Claus footprints by the fireplace.

My favorite time came the night before Christmas when we dressed in our best and had our traditional procession up the stairs and the youngest child placed the Christ Child in the manger. ("Mom always liked you best," one of the siblings always observed to her). It seemed just perfect, and I thought it would always be that way.

Each family member carried a character from our nativity set to be put in place while Daddy played the organ. There was always a big fight over who had to carry the donkey. One year the discussion culminated in a battle that went upstairs and downstairs. Quite a bit of furniture was broken, and the donkey has a badly fractured leg, and we never used it again. Still, I thought we would always have these celebrations. The next summer, my husband died, and of course there could never be the same holiday again

You have to create a holiday that fits who

you are now, and the easiest way, I think, is to have fun with lots of little celebrations instead of one big one.

Some people just seem to know how to make any ordinary day a holiday. Last Sunday at Mass, Fr. Charles Kanai taught us to sing "Thank You, Jesus" in Swahili, his own native language. "Learn a Song in Swahili Day" would be an ideal pre-Thanksgiving holiday.

I've written before about Lenore Clem, the Heart Lady of Fox Island. She's been turning out fat stuffed "feely" hearts 20 years after she started creating them for Mary Bridge Hospital in Tacoma. By now she's sent more than 200,000 hearts around the world to hospitals and special programs from Zambia to Australia. Lenore Clem is 93 years old. She works on her hearts every day, lamenting that it now takes her 15 minutes to make a heart which will comfort a newborn or a child with cancer somewhere in the world. She sits in her big chair and does what she can do, and that's a lot. How about a "Do As Much As You Can Day"?

Years ago at Christmas, I was bedridden in the hospital at Ft. Campbell, KY with a perilously troubled pregnancy. A stranger whose husband served with mine took me home with her and cared for me till my husband returned from taking our older daughter to stay with his parents until the baby came. When I tried to thank her she said, "You can't do anything for me. You'll do it for somebody else." "Do It For Somebody Else Day" would be a fine addition to our new holiday schedule.

Holidays change. We didn't have turkey most Thanksgivings when I was a kid. From about 1943 till several years after World War II there was a turkey shortage and you couldn't get that big bird for your holiday feast, no matter how you tried. "There's turkey at Safeway," someone would call on the party line, and everyone lined up there, usually unsuccessfully. We're not used to seeing lines for food any more, but it was an every day thing then. But mostly dinner had to be something else. One year it was Spam. But mostly it was chicken every Sunday, and we felt lucky to have it. And then one year, there was plenty of turkey and the holiday changed again. Holidays change all the time. We have to change too.

Note #1: Sally Everding taught me two useful phrases in Swahili that will leave us better prepared for any happening:

I particularly like 'Gari langu linaloangama limejaa na mikunga' (my hovercraft is full of eels), and 'Mtu huyu atalipia kila kitu' (This gentleman will pay for everything). Sally writes, "Swahili... a bit of a Bantu/pigeon English... so English phonetic pronunciation works with lots of clicking noises. Several of my work/study helpers at the U of Arkansas were Kenyan or Rwandan... They bickered constantly in Swahili. I got it accepted as an approved language at the university by bringing the students before the language committee (at a reception) and telling the students to proceed with their ongoing argument. No one could dispute that it wasn't a genuine language."

Note#2 – Sadly, Lenore Clem, the Heart Lady, passed away in 2014, but her example of beautiful hearts won't be forgotten.

Thanksgiving - 2010

Thanksgiving Past Tense

Thanksgiving dinners can be very tense. Even one marshmallow less in the candied sweet potatoes will bring howls of protest from diners who will then refuse the dish because they don't like sweet potatoes. It's very hard to change traditions, as I learned the first year my family spent in Taiwan. On Thanksgiving Eve our landlord arrived at the door with his arms full of a large, live, fully befeathered turkey who was apparently really annoyed by the whole proceeding.

"Oh, Mr. Wu--you really shouldn't have done it," I cried very sincerely.

Mr. Wu's beaming smile slowly dimmed. "Easy to fix," he said, making a neck wringing gesture with his hands. Not easy with his arms full of bird. Neither the turkey nor I were convinced. "Don't you Americans like turkey for your holiday--Thanksgiving?" he asked in a puzzled tone. Well yes, but only if it's quietly lying in the butcher's case. Decapitating and plunging the bird into boiling water for plucking was a process I was no more enthusiastic about than the turkey was. I took him from Mr. Wu none too graciously and for Thanksgiving dinner that year we had fried chicken and baked Spam. I can't say it went over well.

Even though that experience convinced me that Thanksgiving is surely the worst day in the whole year to change tradition, I am planning to try something different this holiday. The grandkids are beginning to express an interest in family history. It's about time. So I hope to use the time that we would ordinarily spend critiquing the lifestyles of absent relatives to begin on creating our own family history.

As one of my sons said, "I'm interested in how we came to be who and how we are. But I suppose one big thing, if it's still possible to pin down, is when exactly did our various forebears come to America, and why?"

We're not the only ones who think this is important. Prolific local author Randall Platt told me recently that she believes that there ought to be a law that people must pass on their life stories before they themselves pass on permanently. How would that work? "Say Aunt Clara's been ill for a long time and you pull her off life supports," she explained, "with this law, the doctor runs in and says, 'No, she didn't write her life story. Put her back till she does.'" That may seem impractical, but Author Platt, with nine books to her credit, is firm about the importance of stories. Her latest novel, *Hellie Jondoe*, has won multiple awards, including both the prestigious Willa and the Will Rogers Medallion. She believes it's most important that we all create that sense of where we begin and end. "First, it gives a person a real inventory of their life; every person can see that they have indeed made a difference," she says. "Secondly, a history is something which can be handed down to future generations. What more perfect gift can there be? "

How to get started? I learned from Lakewood historian Cy Happy that sometimes it's easiest to start with one single event. Start with the elders at the table. Ask them to recall their first day of school, or the first Thanksgiving they remember. Who was there? Where did they come from? Who were their parents? Choose a moderator and record everything. Don't get bogged down in the details of what really happened. We do not all remember things the same way. At this point, we'll give the kids a choice between doing research on the computer or doing the dishes. The computer will win. Ancestry.com turns up nuggets in just moments.

It will be a snap to put those stories together in a book. What a great Christmas present! One size fits all. There, your shopping is all done. Don't mention it.

Oh, and what happened to that long ago turkey? Well, we gave him to the tiny lady who collected our garbage into swinging baskets on her shoulders, and she was very pleased. She and our holiday bird were last seen heading over the hill at a turkey trot. I don't know if the turkey became a pet or dinner, but they both looked very happy. Happy Thanksgiving!

Update: It should be noted that Randall Platt now has eleven books to her credit. Her latest, INCOMMUNICADO hits the bookstores as I write this.

Quo Vadis?

I was trying to remove the brand new GPS navigator from the dashboard of my car while I went into church. I didn't really expect that anyone at church would make off with my new prize, but I was trying to form the habit of removing it automatically when I left the car to prevent thefts. It's hard to see why anybody would want my car, but I have the honor to live in one of the car theft meccas of the country, so you can't be sure. When I tried to take the GPS off the dashboard, it came apart in three pieces. I couldn't get them back together.

I sat teary eyed, trying to get the pieces to fit. "Don't panic," I said to myself. "I'm sure these things happen all the time." Of course, I panicked

I have a natural gift for getting lost anywhere I go. I was once lost for three days between Louisville and Nashville. I have been lost in San Francisco. Of course, everybody has been lost in San Francisco. One memorable Sunday, I was lost in my own neighborhood for three hours. That's not easy to do. Only last year I started out to drive some visitors from China to Leavenworth, and instead we ended up in Eastern Washington. My visitors had never seen tumbleweeds before and were very excited. I've sort of enjoyed the thrill of unexpected adventures like that. I just allow a couple of extra hours everywhere I go. So it was with mixed feelings that I received the gift of this ultra-thin widescreen GPS tracking device from my son and his family. The day really went surprisingly well. I didn't break it until the day after Christmas.

Finally I had to call my son and his wife for a tutorial on how to put it all back together. I had to call both of them, because he speaks high tech and she interprets. They showed me how to put the device together and taught me to thoroughly lick the back of the suction cup with my tongue before I put it in on the windshield. I don't know whether that was instruction or revenge, but it did stick nicely. I couldn't find that in the instruction manual, though.

The manual does say not to put the unit in the glove box when it is detached, because that's the first place thieves look. So I stuffed it into my purse, which already weighs as much as a small dog or a large roast. It fits but makes me walk really funny.

Back in the car, I licked the suction cup carefully and stuck it on the windshield. Now I was actually ready to take to the road with my new constant companion, the lady who is the voice of my GPS. I call her Phyllis after my third grade teacher. She doesn't nag, but I'm sure I hear exasperated sighs. I know she's not a local girl from the way she says place names: "Turn onto Neezz-kwaliy," she directs, and "Steel-Laco-om" or "Poi-yallup." I snicker rudely, even though I used to pronounce those place names the same way when I first came here. We arrive safely, but naturally all of this 21st Century magic is not without challenges. I've learned that GPS works by using 31 different government satellites. They pinpoint your locations, but now there's a worry that those very satellites are getting too old and could even fail, leaving us directionless. I'm used to that, but some of you may have to worry a bit.

Today is my 77th birthday. I used to dread birthdays and frequently took to my bed for several days while the family peered at me fearfully, but now I'm tickled to be here. I have a gift card from my daughter for a new birthday suit, much needed. I'm certainly glad I never got a tattoo. My skin has sagged so much it would be down around my ankles now, falling like Larry King's suspenders. I think what I really need is a GPS unit for my life. With nice clear graphics, and easy-to-read maps. I'd just type in the destination--Happiness, Bright Future, Long Life--and Phyllis would take me there. Right, Phyllis?

Never mind. I may get lost on the way, but I can find it myself.

Note: of course, what I didn't know then was that the maps from my GPS would get outdated before the satellites got old, but we're still making the best of it. I also know that my constant companion is not really named Phyllis. Garmin now has more than 200 voices, many of them celebrities available. You can even record and use your own voice, and I was all excited about that, and then I suddenly realized, why would anyone follow directions I gave?

Christmas - 2010

Ten Tips for Handling Holiday Stress

(and they're pretty good the rest
of the year, too)

There isn't much practical help available for controlling holiday stress. I mean, sure, there are plenty of tips for eating healthy, or bringing down your cholesterol level by counting to ten before you kill your spouse--things like that--but what I'm talking about here is real stress, like giving a speech to a large crowd as you realize that your panty hose are crawling slowly down to your knees. Or when you're stuck in a traffic jam on the freeway, and every hazard light in the car comes on. How do you maintain your composure while you decide what to do next? Research shows that if you can find the humor in these situations, or create a little of your own, you'll be able to break the stress spiral and take control again. This is what I mean:

1) Don't fall into the trap of doing what's expected. That will just lead to people expecting more--and we can't have that. Remember that you can't possibly do everything you'd like to do--and as my daughter reminds me, remember there is no such thing as the perfect Christmas. I find it helps to write the three things you really must do tomorrow on a file card. When the morning comes, put your mind in neutral and just do them, and cross them off. When someone tells you to have a nice day, tell them you have other plans. Personally, I like to sigh deeply and say, "I'll try, but I just can't promise."

2) Oh, back to that car with all the lights on. Always carry bubble liquid in your glove compartment. Then, when your car falters to a stop, you simply roll down the window, and blow bubbles. In no time at all, help will arrive, or magically, a path will open through traffic and you'll be able to get out of there.

3) Keep some reliable de-stressing items close at hand, and take "laugh breaks" when you feel tension building up. Remember that every time you laugh, you are actually creating endorphins and breaking the stress cycle. Keep a mirror in the drawer by your phone, where you can pick it up and make faces into it during tense conversations. I have a friend who keeps a big, fluffy pillow and tennis racket at work. When stress accumulates, she simply excuses herself, goes into the other room and spends a happy five minutes beating the stuffing out of the pillow, which she names for her adversary. If the situation is really critical you can draw the offender's face on the pillow with a felt tip pen. Then she returns with a serene smile upon her face, ready to continue.

4) Leaf through *National Geographic* and draw underwear on the Natives. In other words, look at your normal surroundings in a new way.

5) When someone annoys you, stare at them through the tines of a fork, and pretend they are in jail.

6) Smear yourself with caramel and make popcorn with the lid off. At least you'll be able to pinpoint the source of your stress.

7) Bill your doctor for your time spent in his waiting room. This will probably not get you in to see the doctor any sooner, but is immensely satisfying. My favorite technique is that when I check in, I tell the receptionist, "Please tell the doctor that I have an appointment at 2:00 so I'll have to bill him for any time spent after that." Smile prettily. Very satisfying. And I usually get in pretty promptly.

8) Mail yourself an anonymous love letter. (Email doesn't count.) Say all the wonderful things that any observant person would naturally say. When the letter arrives, carry it with you ostentatiously and take it out from time to time with a knowing smile. You can even fan yourself with it occasionally.

9) Practice Reverse Paranoia--the feeling that the world is full of people who are out to do you good. Suspect everyone of having the best intentions toward you. And turn off the TV. Studies show that people who watch TV regularly are much more stressed and fearful and distrustful of others than those who do not.

10) Make a list of resolutions you'd like to get serious about. 1) Exercise. 2) eat less junk food. 3) read more. 4) watch less television. 5) Throw the list away. Keep only resolution Number 5.

The Ghost of Christmas Past

Dorothy Wilhelm was once cast as the Ghost of Christmas Past in a production of Scrooge!. Is that typecasting or what? Dorothy has been an acknowledged spokesperson for people enjoying their second fifty years, for more than three decades. In 1998 she was listed in the *Yearbook of Experts, Authorities and Spokespersons* as an expert on Sex after 50. There it was on page 159 right after Sex Addiction and right before Sex and Love. During that year of interviews, she was asked some very intriguing questions and she concluded that simply having an enthusiasm for a subject and an ability to write about it entertainingly doesn't necessarily make one an expert. After all, she once pursued an elephant into the jungles of Northern Thailand to stop it from running off with her ten year old son. This did not make her an expert on elephants but it certainly made her sensitive to their changing moods. Dorothy is acknowledged by her editors, readers, fellow broadcasters and audiences nation wide as an expert on finding humor in the most unlikely circumstances.

Dorothy Wilhelm was an army wife raising her six children at posts all over the world when she was widowed suddenly at the age of 48. She had less than a year toward her college degree, had never worked outside her home and had no discernible job skills. She could not even drive on the freeway. Faced with a need to make a living, Dorothy did a quick job skills analysis and realized that she possessed the same skills for being a radio talk show host as for working at McDonalds, which is to say, absolutely none. The decision was a no-brainer. "Start at the top." she says, "McDonalds will always be there."

Dorothy started her broadcasting career by talking her way into a five a.m. call in show at a Tacoma radio station so small the signal could best be received from the parking lot . Within a few months she was diagnosed with cancer, so she simply broadcast from home for six months. She soon expanded to KIRO Radio and TV in Seattle one of the largest media markets in the country. She was Creative Living expert for ten years, drawing 500 to 1000 letters per week, from listeners asking for her instructions on how to create home crafts out of items readily found around the house and asking for help with personal problems. She had a Saturday morning show, "Survival Tips" interviewing such guests as the fledgling Martha Stewart . She created humorous drive time spots to distract commuters on the long drive home. At the same time, she began her TV show *50-50, her radio show, Never Too Late, which won two media awards,* and worked on one of the very first national magazines for women past 50.

In 2000, she started her successful TV show, *My Home Town.* Dorothy and crew visited more than a hundred communities in Washington state, showing what's going right in America's small towns. The show ran for more than ten years, was seen in more than a million homes, and was winner of a Beacon Award for excellence in Public Affairs Broadcasting. Her radio show, *Never Too Late* was winner of a Mature Media Award. Her 2009 show, *Never Too Late,* is now available on YouTube. Her newspaper columns began in the Chinese Post in Seattle. They were in English. Her column now, 21 years later, runs locally in the Tacoma News Tribune, *The Olympian,* The Bellingham Herald and in other publications nationally.

A professional speaker on humor and creativity, Dorothy was a founding member of the Pacific Northwest Chapter of the National Speakers Association, and twice won their infrequently awarded Inspirational Award.

Dorothy created a breakfast program for Nordstrom, which increased sales of women's apparel in the Town Square Department by 300% for the day of the performance.

As a working artist, (if you live long enough you get to do everything, she says.) in Bangkok, she parlayed 25 dollars, some macramé yarn and five pounds of dried out clay into a fully staffed recreation service for the Red Cross with two

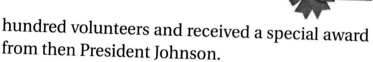

hundred volunteers and received a special award from then President Johnson.

This familiarity with art and artists lends a creative and quirky perspective to her writing as in her story about a spider that crawled under the glass of one of her watercolor paintings - and died. "That's carrying criticism way too far," Wilhelm opined in a newspaper column about the event. She went on to frame column and painting and auctioned both at an Alzheimer's Association fundraiser where it was one of the biggest money makers. It was so successful that other community organizations requested paintings for their fund raisers. Spiders tend to fade away after they die, so she had to keep spray painting these pale little dead spiders black. It was hard on the spiders, but for a good cause.

Dorothy holds a Bachelor's Degree in Communications from Marylhurst University in Oregon. True to her premise that it's never too late; it was awarded when she was 52.

Dorothy's children are successfully grown, and eligible for their own AARP cards. She drives anywhere she wants.

At 80 years of age, Dorothy still loves Christmas and is confident that she is qualified to be an expert now. Anything's possible. Romance? Why not? She caught the elephant after all.

CPSIA information can be obtained at www.ICGtesting.com
Printed in the USA
BVOW03s1909211114

376235BV00003B/5/P

9 780692 329740